St Paul

to

St Nicholas

A handbook for Christian
visitors to Turkey
by
John Hayden

Honey Hill Publishing
St Mary's Church, Honey Hill, Bury St Edmunds, Suffolk IP33 1RT, UK

c 2005 John Hayden and Honey Hill Publishing
First published in 2005 by Honey Hill Publishing

Quotations from the Bible are taken from the New International Version (USA edition) and are used by permission of the copyright holders, the International Bible Society, Colorado Springs, USA.

ISBN 0 9536495 9 8

Honey Hill Publishing is an enterprise of St Mary's Church,
Bury St Edmunds, Suffolk, UK.

Introduction

The purpose of this book is not to provide a guidebook   The main guide-book publishers, such as *Lonely Planet, Rough Guide* and *Baedeker*, cover this aspect.   These books cover such subjects as accommodation and travel, but their description of the various places of interest is very limited. For this aspect it is best to obtain local guides, and the following were the best at time of writing.

Cappadocia by Murat Gulyaz and Irfan Olmez, published by Dunya Turizm Tekstil 2005.

Southern Coast of Turkey, Antalya by Ilhan Aksit, published by Aksit Kultur Turizm 2004, ISBN 975 7039 04 7.

Other specialist guides include:

Hatay: Museum and Environs by Anon, published by Donmez Offset, Ankara, ISBN 975 3870 04 3.

Goreme: Open Air Museum by Murat Gulyaz, published by Demir Color 2003, ISBN 975 9722 70 4.

Pisidian Antioch by Unal Demirer, published by Donmez Offset, Ankara ISBN 975 9271 70 2.

A good book on the background to life in biblical times is to be found in *Backgrounds of Early Christianity* by Everett Ferguson, published by Eerdmans, Grand Rapids, ISBN 0 8028 0669 4. A basic study available is *Daily Life in Ancient Times* by Selcuk Gur, published by Kuyucu Matbaacilik.

The aim of this handbook is to give easily readable information for a Christian visitor.   Often items of specific Christian interest do not receive sufficient attention in the general guide books and it is hoped that this publication will fill the gap without losing the visitor in a mass of detail.

Once more I am deeply indebted to Lance Bidewell for the considerable task he has undertaken in editing this handbook.

Bishop John Hayden
May 2005

Contents

The Graeco-Roman period

At some time in the second millennium BC, a people called the Dorians invaded Greece and drove out large numbers of Ionians. The Ionians then settled in the Aegean islands and the western coast of Asia Minor. Both peoples were of Greek race, so there were Greeks on both sides of the Aegean.

Beyond the Greek coastal settlements lay the kingdom of Lydia (capital, Sardis) and beyond that various peoples of whom the Greeks knew very little. At the end of the sixth century BC Croesus of Lydia ruled over most of the Ionian Greek cities and sent rich gifts to the mainland Greek shrines, hoping to prevent the mainland Greeks from combining with the Ionians against his rule. In 585 BC he went to war against Cyrus of Persia, who had recently extended his territory to the borders of Lydia. He was defeated by Cyrus and the whole of Asia Minor came under Persian rule.

The Persians divided up their empire into satraps, usually ruled by a Persian noble. In 499 BC the Ionians attempted to break free from Persian rule and took Sardis. Darius retaliated by invading Greece. Both he and his successor Xerxes were driven back, and after several other battles in 449 BC the Greeks in Asia Minor obtained semi-autonomy.

The Greeks were still liable to conscription, and we have an interesting insight into life at the time in the writing of Xenophon. He was hired in 401 BC by Cyrus, who was seeking to dethrone the Persian king. Cyrus and all the Greek generals were killed, but Xenophon with others escaped to travel over large areas of present-day Turkey. Xenophon's book, *Anabasis*, opened up for the Greeks the vast expanse of the area.

The southern Greeks regarded the northern Macedonians as barbarians. Philip II, King of Macedonia from 359 to 336, unified Macedonia and built up an army, and was reluctantly appointed by all Greeks to lead an expedition against the Persians to avenge the invasions of Greece. He was assassinated before he started and was succeeded by his son, Alexander, aged 20, who took over Philip's expedition and set out in 334 BC. He crossed the Hellespont and fought the battle of Granicus on

5

the plains of Troy which gave him Asia Minor. He went on to conquer an empire stretching from Egypt and Palestine, across Babylon, through Afghanistan to India. He died of fever at Babylon in 323 BC.

Alexander's policy to Hellenize the East and spread Greek culture succeeded in large areas of western Asia. By the time of Paul, large areas were Greek in thought and education, even though Greece centred on Athens was in steep decline.

After the death of Alexander the empire was divided among his generals. The Antigonid dynasty ruled in Greece, and western Asia was to be a place of conflict between the Seleucids and the Ptolemy dynasty based in Egypt.

In 191 BC the Seleucid Antiochus the Great attempted to free the Greeks from Roman rule by invading Greece. He was defeated and Roman influence spread into Asia. At first the Romans ruled by strengthening the Kingdom of Pergamum. In 133 BC Attalus III of Pergamum died and bequeathed his kingdom to the Romans.

The Romans divided the area of Turkey into the provinces of Asia, Bithynia and Pontus, Galatia, Lycia, Pamphylia, Cappadocia and Cilicia. Each had a governor and paid taxes to Rome. For nearly three hundred years there was a time of great prosperity and peace, but towards the end of the third century AD the seeds of later weaknesses were beginning to show. After some major reorganization the empire was divided and Diocletian took the Asian part. He began another severe persecution of the Christians.

In 323 AD Constantine took control of the whole empire, and made Byzantium, which he renamed Constantinople, his capital. He rewarded the Christians who had been on his side against their persecutors Diocletian and Licinius. From that time until the Islamic invasion, bishops increasingly held power within local government as the central government went into terminal decline.

6

Graeco–Roman town planning

The first record of town planning was in 3000 BC when the Egyptian city of Kahum was built to house the men who worked on the pyramids. The streets were straight and laid out in rectangular blocks.

By 500 BC city planning was not an unusual procedure. Plans for several Greek cities show radial arteries superimposed on a rectangular system in a fan-shaped design. This form is now used in many countries as a basis for planning new towns.

The Roman town in the provinces was planned round a central forum close to, but separated from, the crossing of two main roads which normally ran north–south and east–west. Less important roads ran at right angles to the main roads. Adherence to this gridiron pattern was so persistent that not infrequently the Romans levelled uneven land to allow straight-line development. They also attempted to segregate industry, and in Rome the height of buildings was limited.

The forum was surrounded by a colonnade and the principal buildings — temples, basilica, senate house and covered market — such was the emphasis put on this central area in both Greek and Roman planning, or more correctly, civic design.

Growing complexity of government in the independent cities of the Greco-Roman world necessitated special buildings to be built round the forum. In the bouleuterion, or council hall, were the legislative and executive functions. Nearby stood the prytaneum, in which was the 'eternal' fire, the official symbol of state unity. Here banquets were held and the General had his residence. Courts were usually held in the colonnades round the forum, the stoa, and even in the theatre.

In both civilizations government still retained its ancient connection with religious rites. The Roman temples differed in many important respects from those of the Greeks. Instead of the comparatively low stylobate, with its three steps all round, the Romans substituted a high platform, or podium, with a flight of steps on the entrance facade. Also, while Greek temples are isolated from other buildings and almost always face east–west, those of the Romans usually face the forum or are placed at the end of a street to close a vista, their orientation being governed by their relation to other buildings. This results in an emphasis on the entrance facade, with an increased depth to the portico.

During the later Greek period the agora (market place) became a formally enclosed rectangle rather than the picturesque group of colonnades and public buildings. The roads outside the city gates were lined with an ever-increasing variety of sarcophagi.

Baths were a key feature of Roman life and they were of two types: the balnae, a type of Turkish bath with rooms at different temperatures, and therma, an establishment of great magnificence with facilities for every gymnastic exercise; along with halls for philosophers, poets and rhetoricians. The planning of the therma was governed by axial planning and the grouping of all subsidiary halls and rooms round a great central hall.

Roman private houses were also of two types: the domus and insula. The domus consisted of suites of rooms grouped round a central hall and was more common in the cities of the eastern Mediterranean. The insulae, or blocks of flats several stories high, were regarded as far too dangerous for an area prone to earthquakes.

Greek Architecture 700–146 BC

Greek architecture of the Hellenic Period has long been recognized as the most beautiful building form yet devised by man. The essentially simple column and beam method of construction formed the basis of this style of architecture, which was used for all temples and important public buildings. This style is thought to have been derived from timber construction methods. The columns, beams and other components were stylized and refined by succeeding generations of artists and craftsmen to a degree which has rarely been equalled and never surpassed in the building forms of subsequent ages.

Marble was readily available for constructing the most important buildings, and the natural beauty of this material, carved with great skill into the structurally pure and well proportioned forms of Greek temples glistening white under cloudless Mediterranean skies, must have afforded a sight of awesome beauty, making it easy to believe that the gods had made their homes on earth.

Greek temples, although basically similar in general shape and construction, nevertheless differed in detail and ornament. Three main types are evident: namely the Doric, Ionic and Corinthian Orders. These are chiefly distinguished from each other by the proportions of the columns and the shapes of the column tops or capitals.

The earliest, simplest and most robust style is the Doric, with examples dating from 640 BC. The most famous temple built in this style is the Parthenon at Athens, constructed in the period from 447 to 432 BC.

The Ionic Order, with examples dating from 560 BC, has columns of a more slender proportion than the Doric and can easily be identified by the remarkable volute, or scroll, design of the capitals.

The Corinthian dates from 420 BC. The slender columns are topped by an inverted bell shape surrounded by acanthus leaves.

Roman Architecture 146 BC–AD 365

Roman architecture owes much to the Greeks and also the Etruscans who were the original inhabitants of Central Italy. Their architecture, dating from about 750 BC, is specially notable for the use of the radiating arch, and the Romans continued to use this form combined with the column and beam favoured by the Greeks. This combination of columns and beams with arches and vaults gives Roman architecture its own distinctive character.

The Doric, Ionic and Corinthian Orders continued to be used by the Romans, who also added two other types, namely the Tuscan and the Composite. The Tuscan is a simplified version of the Doric with an unfluted shaft, simple moulded capital and plain entablature. The Composite has a capital which is a combination of the Corinthian and Ionic types and was often used in triumphal arches to give an ornate character.

Temples were the predominant buildings of the Greeks and were of one storey, but the complex civilization and varied needs of the Romans demanded other buildings, often of several storeys. Thermae (baths), temples, amphitheatres, aqueducts, bridges, tombs and basilicas all testify to the great constructive ability of the Romans, whose majestic buildings were in accord with the grandeur of Roman Imperial power.

The Romans invented a form of concrete which they used to great effect and economy in the construction of walls, vaults and domes. Brick, stone, marble and mosaic were still used, but only as facing materials. Mosaics were used not only on walls but on floors and are of great variety. Statues housed in niches in walls were much in use as decoration.

Temples were similar in general form to Greek temples, although half columns attached to the side walls often took the place of the surrounding colonnade of the Greeks. Roofs were often vaulted. They were generally sited to face onto the public open space or forum. A few temples, such as the famous Pantheon in Rome, were built in circular form.

10

Basilicas were halls of justice and commercial exchange. The usual plan of a basilica was a rectangle twice as long as its width. Two or four rows of columns divided the interior into three or five aisles. The tribunal was at the far end on a raised dais, set in a semicircular apse around which were ranged seats for the assessors. The basilica form is interesting, in that it was adopted by the early Christians as a pattern for church buildings, after Christianity was permitted as a public religion in the fourth century AD.

Remains of buildings dating from the Roman period are to be found at many of the ancient city sites of Asia Minor and Greece.

Greek Capitals.

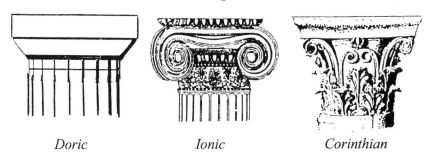

Doric   *Ionic*   *Corinthian*

Roman capitals

Corinthian   *Composite*

11

Byzantine Architecture AD 324 onwards

The dome, which had always been traditional in the east, became the dominant design feature of Byzantine architecture, which was a fusion of domed with columnar construction. Domes of brick, stone or concrete were supported on pendentives over square compartments, whereas in Roman architecture the use of a dome was limited to compartments of circular or polygonal shape. The use of the dome as the main constructional element governed the plan form of Byzantine churches, which usually consist of a central square space covered by a dome on pendentives and surrounded by short arms on each side to give a cross-shaped plan, the remaining corners being often filled in to complete a square.

An entrance vestibule or narthex was built onto one side to give access to the church, while at the opposite end a semicircular recessed area or apse housed the altar, which was partitioned off from the main body of the church by a screen or iconostasist.

Domes or semi-domes were sometimes used to cover the subsidiary parts of Byzantine churches in addition to the central space. In order to withstand the thrust from the domes, the walls were solidly constructed of brick or stone, with exterior decoration taking the form of banding patterns. Internally, the large areas of wall and dome surface were decorated by marble, glass mosaic and wall paintings. The interior of a Byzantine church was one vast visual aid, illustrating Bible events and Christian doctrine in rich and glowing colours. Figure sculpture was not allowed by the Greek Church as it was regarded as idolatry.

Windows were small, making the interior restful and cool in contrast to the glaring eastern sunshine outside. An encircling ring of windows, set in the base of the dome, was often the chief source of light for the church. Columns were used to support galleries, and in early buildings these were often obtained from existing ancient buildings. When new columns were used, the capitals were of designs developed from the Greek or Roman types, or a new pattern such as the cushion, bird or basket.

The key characteristic of Byzantine ornament is that the pattern is incised rather than raised.

The Byzantine style of architecture was adopted by the Orthodox Church as being eminently suitable for the unchanging forms of its liturgy, and as such has continued as a traditional building type right down to the present day.

Good examples of Byzantine architecture are on the hill of the 1001 churches near Derbe, and Kilistra near Lystra.

Three examples of Byzantine capitals

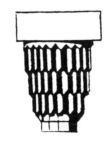

An Islamic-style capital

Islamic Architecture AD 1453 onwards

When the Ottoman Turks captured Byzantium they inherited a number of impressive churches. These were converted for use as mosques and also served as patterns for new mosques.

The great mosques of Istanbul, built from the sixteenth century onwards, were modelled on the Hagia Sophia, Istanbul which was already 1,000 years old by this time.

Ornament in mosques and other Islamic buildings was strictly regulated by the rules of the Koran, which prohibited the copying of natural objects. In consequence, forms of decoration were developed based on elaborate geometric designs and using brilliant colouring in red, white, blue, silver and gold. Often quotations from the Koran in Arabic script were used as decoration, in the form of tiled panels. In contrast to Greek architecture, which was essentially very simple in form, Islamic architecture is characterized by the intricacy and restlessness of the elaborate geometric ornament, used both internally and externally in mosques and other important buildings.

Fountains, which are often roofed over, are to be found in the forecourts of mosques and in public squares.

Turbes (tombs) are of a unique shape and are to be found near mosques. The Tekke of Mevlana at Konya (Iconium) was the convent of the Whirling Dervishes who performed wild ritual dances. It is now an Islamic museum and contains many interesting objects such as relics, garments, Korans, embroidered brocades and carpets, etc. The turbe of Mevlana Celaleddin, the founder of the Whirling Dervishes, is within the building complex. The marble sarcophagus is covered in brocade.

14

Antioch

Antioch was given this name in 300 BC by Seleucus I Nicator, one of Alexander the Great's generals and the son of Antiochus. (In New Testament times there were at least sixteen other places bearing the same name, one of which was Antioch in Pisidia.) It was sited on the left bank of the river Orontes, about 12 miles from the sea (now 20 miles) in a fertile plain which separates the Lebanon mountains in the south from the Taurus to the north-west.

In the early stone age it was inhabited by the Prototigris who, by the early third millennium BC, were ruled by the Akads. Later it was part of the Yamhat Kingdom based at Aleppo.

It was a free city under Hittite rule and continued to retain this independence, even after the fall of the Hittite empire in 1190 BC.

In 841 BC the Assyrians controlled the plain until the Persians took it in 538 BC. Then in 333 BC Alexander the Great brought Persian rule in the region to an end and opened the way for the Selucids to develop the settlement. In 317 BC Antigonus began to build a town to the north on one of the tributaries of the Orontes. However, after his defeat in 311 BC by Seleucus at Issios, this settlement was abandoned. Seleucus began developing a site on the slopes of Mt Silpius. He was able to link his town with an abundant supply of water from the springs of Daphne, five miles to the south. He also founded the port of Seleucia, where the Orontes flowed into the Mediterranean.

The city grew rapidly and became the administrative hub for the whole region. It was laid out on the plans of Alexandria, with two great colonnaded streets intersecting at the centre. Future rulers built a walled town in each of the quarters and so it was also called Tetrapolis. In 148 BC it was almost totally destroyed by an earthquake.

A new, far more splendid city arose from the rubble and continued to grow in wealth and influence. So when Rome took over the region in 64 BC it became the capital for the large province of Syria which

15

stretched down to Egypt and to the desert in the east, even though it was at the extreme north-west of the territory.

The city had a mixed population. Amongst this was a large wealthy Jewish section which carried considerable influence in the city affairs. The Romans invested heavily in the city and it soon became one of the wonders of the Roman world. By 42 BC Antioch was the third largest city in the Roman world (after Rome and Alexandria) and was to retain its prominence for several centuries to come.

It is described with great pride by Libanius. 'Every district of the city provides bathing establishments — there is no lack of water. The public fountains flow for ornament since every one has water within his doors. With us night is distinguished from day only by the difference of the lighting.' Bringing together the various descriptions that are available to us, the following picture emerges.

The city was laid out in the gridiron pattern. Its two intersecting main streets were about four and a half miles long, with a central road for horses pulling chariots or carts and each side a covered colonnade paved with marble. Each side was lined with public buildings, markets, temples, statues and fountains. At night the whole area was lit by thousands of lights which extended along the ten-mile street of pleasure with its thousands of dancing girls.

Passion for the theatre and racecourse was proverbial. One theatre presented an old Greek tragedy of the Trojan War in five scenes, displaying shipbuilding, the launch of the fleet, the voyage, with the dolphins playing in the water around the vessels, and finally a storm at sea, with thunder and lightning, amid which the boats sank to the bottom.

Technology was utilized in the homes of the rich, who had such inventions as an automatic door opener, a washing machine which delivered water and soap as needed, water sprinklers, tap water and central heating.

16

Antioch and Paul

Paul, like most of his fellow Jews, would not have found the lifestyle of Antioch compatible with his upbringing and faith. It was a city which worshipped wealth, pleasure and sex. It seemed full of tipsters, mediums, dancers, actors, and many who were only too ready to engage in mockery. The Emperor Julian was later to call them the 'beard mockers'. It can have been no surprise to Paul that the followers of Jesus were mockingly first called Christians in that city.

Josephus records that the Jewish population was around 50,000 — a considerable proportion of the estimated 300,000. They enjoyed the privileges of a politeuma within the free city. So they were able to keep the Sabbath and other Jewish regulations and were exempt from military service.

Into this city Greek-speaking Jewish Christians fled from the persecution in Jerusalem. They began to preach to the Greek-speaking Gentiles who attended the synagogue, as well as to their own people. One of these converts to Judaism may have been Nicolas, one of the seven deacons chosen in Acts 6:5.

Following the success of the early preachers, Barnabas collected Paul from Tarsus to help with the work there (Acts 11:25). Among the church leaders, besides Barnabas and Paul, were Simeon called Niger (black), Lucius of Cyrene, and Manaen (who had been brought up with Herod). Probably Jewish Christians and Gentiles met separately for worship, maybe the Jews meeting on Saturday and the Gentiles on Sunday. About AD 46 the community sent famine relief to Jerusalem, and the Council of Jerusalem (Acts 15) produced a ruling over how far Gentiles were to keep the Torah.

Paul made Antioch his headquarters, but evidence is weak that Peter became its first bishop. Indeed Galatians 2:11 seems to suggest that Peter's presence there was far from harmonious, as he seems to have encouraged the separation between Jew and Gentile which had been abandoned in the city following the Jerusalem ruling.

17

John Stott, in his commentary on Acts 13, raises the following questions.

First, to whom did the Holy Spirit reveal his will? Who is the 'they' who were worshipping and fasting, and to whom he spoke? ... It is probable that the church members as a whole are in mind, since both they and the leaders are mentioned together in verse 1, and on the not dissimilar occasion when the seven were to be chosen, it was the local church as a whole who acted (6:2–6). Moreover, when Paul and Barnabas returned, 'they gathered the church together'. They reported to the church because they had been commissioned by the church (14:26–27)....

Secondly, what was it that the Holy Spirit revealed to the church? It was very vague. The nature of the work to which he had called Barnabas and Saul was not specified. It was not unlike the call of Abram. To him God had said, 'Go to the land I will show you.'... In both cases the call to go was clear, while the land and the work were not. So in both cases the response to God's call required an adventurous step of faith.

Thirdly, how was God's call disclosed? We are not told. The most likely guess is that God spoke to the church through one of the prophets. But his call could have been inward rather than outward, that is, through the Spirit's witness in their hearts and minds. However it came to them, their first reaction was to fast and pray, partly (it seems) to test God's call and partly to intercede for the two who were to be sent out.... Then, *after they had fasted and prayed,* and so assured themselves of God's call and prepared themselves to obey it, *they placed their hands on them and sent them off.* This was ... a valedictory commissioning to missionary service.

Who, then, commissioned the missionaries? Would it not be true to say both that the Spirit sent them out, by instructing the church to do so, and that the church sent them out, having been directed by the Spirit to do so? This balance will be a healthy corrective to opposite extremes. The first is the tendency to individualism, by which a Christian claims direct personal guidance by the Spirit without any reference to the church. The second is the tendency to institutionalism, by which all decision-making is done by the church without any reference to the Spirit ... Still today it is the responsibility of every local church to be sensitive to the Holy Spirit, in order to discover whom he may be gifting and calling.

(Excerpts from J.R.W.Stott, *Message of Acts*, The Bible Speaks Today [Leicester:IVP,1990], pp.216f.).

18

Antioch in the early church

While no direct reference is made in the New Testament to any of its books being written in Antioch, it is possible that the Gospel of Matthew and Paul's letter to the Galatians came from there.

In almost fifty years from AD 252 to 300, as many as ten assemblies of the church were held at Antioch. At the Council of Nicea, Antioch still retained its third place after Rome and Alexandria. The Antioch Synod in AD 341 passed the 25 canons which became the basis of ecclesiastical law throughout Christendom. So strong was the church there, that by the end of the fourth century Chrysostom reckoned 100,000 Christians were living in the city — about half of its population.

The Antiochene text of the Greek New Testament was one of the most important building blocks in the preservation of the Scriptures.

Ignatius (AD 35–107), the Bishop of Antioch, strongly supported Paul's views against Judaizing tendencies. He also condemned the heresies which denied the full humanity of Jesus. However, after him a number of Gnostic Christians were connected with the church at Antioch. Among them were Menander, Saturninus, Tatian and Axionicus.

Its theologians, Basil the Great, Theodore and Theodoret, were household names in the fourth century. Their theology, linked in certain ways with the gnostic teachings, was a seedbed for Nestorianism (thought to involve a separation between the divine nature and the human) and Monophysitism (Christ had only a single divine nature, clad in human flesh). Athanaeius of Alexandria won the hearts of orthodoxy with his doctrine of the person of Christ (giving equal weight to both human and divine natures), popularly laid out in the Athanaesian creed, and as a result the position of Antioch in the early church fell into terminal decline.

In the fifth century the hermit Simon Stylites lived on his pillar forty miles to the east, and his body was brought to Antioch for burial.

Four earthquakes in the sixth century killed 250,000 or more residents and left the city in ruins. It was plundered by the Persians and suffered a severe outbreak of plague.

By the time of the Arab Islamic invasion of 638, Antioch was a small town of less than 10,000 people. It never rose again above that number until the middle of the twentieth century.

In 1097, after a siege of nine months, it was captured by the Crusaders. Muslim armies tried several times to retake until it fell to the Mamelukes. Mongols captured it in 1260 and held it for seven years. In 1560 it was captured by the Ottoman Turks. After World War 1 it came under French rule until Turkey captured it again in 1938.

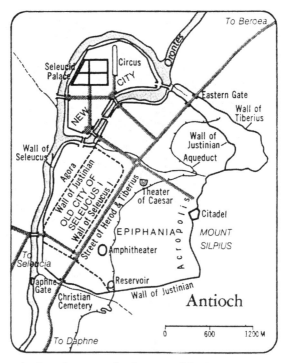

A plan showing the layout of the Roman city

Antioch today

Antakya, in Hatay region, is situated on the Asi River (Orontes).

The museum houses one the richest collections of Roman mosaics in the world. These mosaics come from the villas of ancient Antioch and Daphne. The museum is open Tuesday to Sunday from 8.30 am to 12 noon and 1.30pm to 5pm.

Also in the city are the Roman bridge and the mosque of Habib Haccar which was once a church. About twenty fourth-century churches have been unearthed.

On the outskirts of the city is St Peter's Grotto. The cave church is supposed to be the place where Peter preached, and was declared a holy place by the Vatican in 1983. It was certainly used as a church by the Crusaders, who in 1098 built the west wall and narthex. There are some fresco and mosaic remains near the altar. A narrow tunnel runs from the church through the hillside away from the town and may have been an escape route.

The Iron Gate of Antioch is close to the grotto among the city ruins. The Castle of Antioch provides an interesting panoramic view.

Five miles to the south at Harbiye is the place where Apollo is said to have fallen in love with Daphne, but Mother Earth, in order to save Daphne, turned her into an elegant tree. The site which was the source of Antioch's water supply is still full of trees, orchid gardens and waterfalls.

A mosaic in the Museum of Hatay

Seleucia

The port of Antioch is one of at least ten cities named after the founder of the Seleucid dynasty. To clarify, Seleucia on the Orontes was called Seleucia Pieria. The Seleucids used it as their capital for the region until Antioch was seen to provide a better location.

This port city and fortress was five miles inland from the Syrian coast on the Orontes River. It served as the seaport for the city of Antioch, which lay about sixteen miles further upstream. It was from Seleucia that Paul and Barnabas sailed for Cyprus on their first missionary journey (Acts 13:4). In describing their return, Acts 14:26 states that 'they sailed back to Antioch'; but it is highly probable that they would have needed to leave the ship at Seleucia and continue to Antioch by land. When Barnabas sailed to Cyprus a second time with Mark, he must have boarded ship in Seleucia again (15:39).

Seleucia was built by Seleucus Nicator in the early third century BC. It had great military significance in the struggles between the Seleucids and the Ptolemies of Egypt. Ptolemy III Euergetes captured it in the middle of the third century, but in 219 BC it was regained by Antiochus III the Great. According to I Maccabees 11:8, the city passed back into the hands of Egypt in 146 BC when Ptolemy VI sought to re-establish Egyptian control over the Syro-Palestinian sea coast. At one time Seleucia served as a refuge for Cleopatra. In 108 BC it became independent and remained so even after Pompey's conquest of Syria in 64 BC. Its status as a free city was confirmed in AD 70. It was the base for an imperial fleet throughout the first century.

The ancient city of Seleucia was built on the rocky slope of a spur of the Amanus Mountains, Mt Pierius, known now as Jebel Musa (Musa Dagi). The site was so favourable for a frontier fortress that Seleucia has been called a 'Syrian Gibraltar'. The city extended in a narrow strip up the mountain slope and was surrounded by a wall four miles in perimeter. A natural moat was formed by two mountain streams flowing outside the walls on the east and on the west. Originally the stream on the west terminated inside the city in the inner harbour, but it posed such a threat when flooded that the Romans built a remarkable canal to divert it. This excavation, still visible, is nearly one mile long, twenty feet wide and twenty feet high. Two sections were tunnelled through the mountain; one contains the inscription *Divus Vespasianus et Divus Titus* (Divine Vespasian and Divine Titus), suggesting that it was constructed around AD 70.

The port, the business district, and the suburbs are in the lower city, from which a winding stairway cut into the rock leads to the upper city. The ruins of the amphitheatre, a paved area that may have been the agora, and a large Doric temple, are in the upper city.

From the Antioch Gate a road led to that city along the north side of the river. The acropolis is 1,000 feet above sea level and is well fortified. Many of the city's residents were sailors or fishermen. Wine was produced in the surrounding territory.

Efforts to maintain the harbour proved unsuccessful, since silt deposited by the Orontes River turned it into a marshland. So by the fifth century AD the site was abandoned. Iskenderun, to the north, is now the main port for the area.

It is still possible to trace the walls of the inner harbour, the canal through which ships passed from the outer to the inner harbour, as well as various ruins of temples, and theatres in the upper town. However, the upper town is a stiff climb up the mountain, and when there, it is difficult to work out what is what!

As the site is well off the tourist route, just north of the modern town of Samandag, little has been done to make it user friendly!

St Ignatius

Ignatius' date of birth is unknown. Some put it as early as AD 35 and others as late as AD 50. Likewise the date of his martyrdom varies between AD 98 and 117. The key matter of importance is that in Ignatius we have an early Christian who lived at the time of, and quite likely met, some of the early apostles. He wrote seven letters (Ephesus, Magnesia, Tralles, Rome, Philadelphia, Smyrna, and to Polycarp) which give us insight into the teaching of the church in the immediate post-apostolic age.

We know nothing for certain of his life until, in his ninth year as Bishop of Antioch, he was brought before Trajan to explain why he had opposed the edict for all citizens to unite in the worship of the gods. It may well have been that someone in the community reported him and the Romans were forced to take action as there is no widespread report of persecution at that time. He gave a strong and courageous defence, but Trajan ordered him to be shipped to Rome for the amphitheatre. He commented, 'I am God's wheat, and I am being ground by the teeth of the beasts so that I may appear as pure bread.'

His journey to Rome was far from easy. Most of it was overland, but at one stage he seems to have been bound in the hold of the ship with ten leopards! He travelled overland from Tarsus or Antalya to Smyrna, and made use of the route chosen by his guards to visit Laodicea, Philadelphia and Sardis, only a few years after John had sent to them the letters of Revelation. There may have been a delay at Smyrna which enabled him to meet with representatives of other churches like Ephesus. His guards, thinking of him as just another prisoner, must have been astonished when, in place after place, the Christians led by their bishop came to visit him. After embarking at Troas, he landed in Macedonia and continued on by land and sea to his destination. He seems to have been martyred very soon after his arrival in Rome.

In his letters Ignatius deals with several key issues of his day. The Judaizers had not been thwarted by the Council of Jerusalem, and the church was under constant pressure from them. He points out in his letter to the Magnesians, 'It is absurd to talk Jesus Christ and to practise Judaism. After all, Judaism believed in Christianity, not Christianity in

Judaism.' He also remarks that Christians are 'no longer keeping the Sabbath, but living a life ruled by the Lord's day, whereon our life too had its rising through him'. He hardly mentions the Old Testament, but knew well, and quotes from, many of the New Testament writings, which is a very clear sign of their very early acceptance within the church.

Another major concern was with the Docetists. H. M. Gwatkin points out that 'The stumbling block of that age was not so much the Lord's divinity as his crucifixion. Because he suffered, said the Jew, he was not divine. Because he was divine, replied the Gnostics, he did not suffer In either case, it is denied that the Redeemer suffered at all.'

Ignatius writes, 'Jesus Christ, was of the race of David, the child of Mary, who was truly born, and ate and drank, was truly persecuted under Pontius Pilate, was truly crucified and died, before the eyes of those in heaven and those on earth and those under the earth; who also was truly raised from the dead, since the Father raised him up, who in like manner will also raise up us who believe on him.'

He had a strong conviction for the need of church unity and holiness among believers. He promoted the bishop as the focal point of such unity but there is no hint of such authority being handed down to him from the apostles. For Ignatius, the key quality for a bishop and his clergy was their relationship to the will of God in Christ. His writings contain the first recorded mention of all Christians as the catholic church. 'When you meet frequently, the forces of Satan are nullified and his destructive power is cancelled in the unity of your faith.' So faith and love are to be foremost among Christians. He points out to the Ephesians that faith is the beginning, and the end is love, and the two coming together in unity are God, and all the rest that makes for good conduct follows from them.The new life has to be lived in the principle that, thanks to our union with Christ, God is dwelling in us. What does it mean to live in faith and love? Ignatius lists the following: true belief, unity in the church, moral purity, good relations within the church and with outsiders, such as forbearance.

Tarsus

Tarsus is mentioned in the New Testament as the place where Paul was born, of which he was a citizen, and where he spent some time after his conversion before Barnabas arrived to seek his help in Antioch. We do not hear about a Christian church or of Paul spending time there as part of his missionary journeys, although he passed by several times.

The Cydnus river flowed through the centre of the town, and its cool swift waters were the boast of the city. Around it was the fertile plain of Cilicia. It began as a Hittite and Ionian settlement but grew in importance under the Assyrians. The city is mentioned on the Black Obelisk (850 BC). The Tarshish mentioned in Psalm 72:10 and elsewhere in the Old Testament was on the shores of the Red Sea, either in Arabia or Africa.

Its assets were its extensive and safe harbour; its rich farming lands; and being at the foot of the main pass through the Taurus mountains to the north — the Cilician Gates. Its two great engineering works were the harbour and the road. Its harbour had been created out of the Rhegma, a natural lagoon. Its road up through the Cilician Gates had been a stream bed which engineers had widened to allow a wagon to pass through.

Tarsus was most accessible from the sea or from the east. Even after the Cilician Gates were cut, crossing the Taurus was a difficult operation for an invading army, as Xenophon and Arrian show.

After the Assyrian power decayed, princes, several of whom bore the name or title Syennesis, ruled Tarsus. Under Persian power it was governed by satraps. When in the year 401 BC the younger Cyrus marched against Babylon, the city was governed by King Syennesis in the name of the Persian monarch. Tarsus was already Greek and had a tendency to become more and more Hellenized. In the fourth century BC Alexander took Tarsus without a fight, even the Cilician Gates being left unguarded. But he nearly died of a fever when, feeling the heat of the coastal plain, he bathed in the cold waters of the Cyndus.

The Seleucids followed, and it was made a free city by Antiochus IV Epiphanes in 171 BC. He conferred citizenship on a number of the Jewish residents and possibly Paul's forebears. They may also have grown in importance in the city and been given Roman citizenship by one of the great Romans who visited the city: Pompey, Cicero (governor 51 BC), Julius Caesar, Antony or Augustus.

The event for which Tarsus is most remembered may well have been witnessed by Paul's father. Cleopatra had sailed from Egypt to Tarsus, where Antony was resting after the triumphal tour that followed his victory at Philippi. He had sent for the Queen of Egypt to punish her for the aid she gave to Cassius. Cleopatra, knowing how sternly he punished and fined his enemies, decided to make the sensational appearance which Plutarch and Shakespeare have immortalised. When the Egyptian fleet came in from the sea and entered the lake of Rhegma, Antony, sitting on his throne in the marble streets of Tarsus, noticed that the crowds had melted away   leaving him alone. They had gone to watch the approaching pageant. They saw a vessel with a gilded stern, sails of purple outspread, and silver oars moving in time to the sound of flutes, pipes and harps. Dressed like Aphrodite, the Goddess of Love, Cleopatra lay beneath an awning bespangled with gold, while boys like painted Cupids stood on each side, fanning her. At the helm and at the rigging stood her most beautiful slave women in the guise of Nereids and Graces. The crowds on the river bank could smell the perfumes burning on the ship. Antony fell for her charms. He was soon to fall from power and Julius Caesar took on the role as her lover.

Such visits under Roman rule made Tarsus one of the greatest cities of the east It was not to last. As early as the sixth century it became impossible to reach Tarsus by ship. At that time Justinian cut an artificial channel to the east of the city to alleviate disastrous flooding. By 1432 all that was left was a tiny stream. Soon the harbour became silted and a marshland — a breeding place for mosquitoes.

Tarsus — a place of learning

Its fame as a centre of learning predated Roman times and continued on through them.

The enthusiasm with which it had taken up Greek education and civilization had made it one of the three great university cities of the Mediterranean world. Strabo speaks of the Tarsian university as even greater than those of Athens and Alexandria; and he observes that all the students were from the area, yet also many from Tarsus could be found in universities throughout the world. Demetrius, as Plutarch tells us, went to Britain and Egypt. Athenodorus, the Stoic, was the companion of Cato the younger, and died in his house. Another Stoic, Athenodorus Kananites, was the teacher of Augustus.

Athenodorus retired to Tarsus in his old age, greatly honoured by his pupil Augustus, and invested by him with extraordinary authority in the city, which he set about reforming by linking citizenship with wealth. His rule was followed by another Tarsian philosopher named Nestor, who also had won favour with Augustus. Their doctrines may be taken as those which most influenced Tarsus in the time of Paul. Paul may have studied in Tarsus before moving to Jerusalem to become a pupil of Gamaliel. However, most scholars interpret Acts 22:3 to mean he moved to Jerusalem in his childhood. His quotation from Aratus (Acts 17:28) may have come from further studies between his conversion and his move to Antioch.

Here are some quotations from Nestor's teaching:

> So live with men as if God saw; so speak with God as if men were listening too.
> The student lives well, not by renouncing humanity and society, but by drawing friends round himself. He who lives and studies for his own sole benefit will fall into mere misuse of the time which nature requires us to spend.
> One must be able to give an account of one's time and prove one's old age by the amount of what one has done for the good of the world, and not simply by the length of time one has lived.

Tarsus after Paul

Tarsus in the early church never assumed great importance. We read of its two principal churches, St Peter's and St Paul's, but little remains of these.

The first bishop, Helenus, dates from the third century; he went several times to Antioch in connection with the dispute concerning Paul of Samosata. Among its other bishops are Lupus, present at the Council of Ancyra in 314; Theodorus, at that of Nicaea in 325; Helladius, condemned at Ephesus, and who appealed to the pope in 433; and above all the celebrated exegete Diodorus, teacher of Theodore of Mopsuestia and consequently one of the fathers of Nestorianism. From the sixth century the metropolitan See of Tarsus had seven suffragan bishoprics. The Greek archdiocese is again mentioned in the tenth century .

Owing to the importance of Tarsus many martyrs were put to death there, among them being St Pelagia, St Boniface, St Marinus, St Diomedus, and Sts Cerycus and Julitta. Several later Roman emperors were interred there — Tacitus, Maximinus Daza, and Julian the Apostate.

The Arabs took possession of Tarsus from the seventh century and kept it until 965, when Nicephorus Phocas annexed it again to the Byzantine Empire. This union continued for nearly a century. The Crusaders captured it again from the Turks in 1097, and it became part of the kingdom of Lesser Armenia until about 1350. There was still an Armenian presence in the town when it was sold to the Egyptians. Since then Tarsus has been under Islamic rule.

Tarsus today

The 'Roman or Cleopatra gate' and bridge come from a period well after Paul's time. The gate was restored in the mid-1990s.

The house of Paul is obviously not genuine, but the well may have a greater claim. Wells can often have ancient beginnings, so there may be some evidence for its use in Pauline times. The area has been cleared to provide an interesting site for visitors.

The so-called 'tomb of Seth, son of Noah' may have been a pagan or Christian shrine, and there are various foundations of temples or later Christian churches. The foundations of the hippodrome are beneath the American School and those of the theatre below a primary school.

The Eski Cami, an old mosque, may have been a church in Crusader times and been dedicated to St Paul. It is beside a former Roman bath house.

The sixteenth-century Mehmet Efendi Medresesi now houses the Tarsus Museum.

There is a cave of the 'seven sleepers' to the north. A similar cave exists at Ephesus and probably refers to a pagan myth predating Christianity.

The Roman arch at Tarsus

Cappadocia

Heroditus tells us that the name Cappadocia comes from the Persian and means the land of the well-bred or beautiful horses (Katpatuka). At first the name referred to a much wider area, including Pontus, but later it was divided up and Cappadocia became roughly what it is now: bordered in the south by the Taurus mountains, in the east by the river Euphrates, in the north by Pontus, and in the west, rather vaguely, by the central desert. Most of Cappadocia is 1,000 metres above sea level.

Today, centred on the triangle of Nevsehir, Urgup and Avanos, Cappadocia is in the middle of a once-active volcanic region. At that time, in the Pliocene era, these volcanic eruptions were so strong that the lava in some places was up to 100 metres thick. Over the years, volcanoes, wind, rain and ice sculpted the landscape from the lava, ash, clay, sandstone and marl.   As the land eroded, the basalt stones remained and formed conical structures sometimes reaching as high as 45 metres. The local people called these unique rock formations 'Fairy Chimneys'. Man has also played his part by carving the rocks. He built houses, churches and over 120 underground cities. The largest of these, Ozkonak, once had a population of sixty thousand. The canyon formed by the Melendiz stream, which has pierced its way through the rocks, is called the Ihlara Valley. In this eight-mile long valley there are 105 churches and 4,535 houses.

Some layers are softer than others, and thus water penetrates deeper in the soil, leaving a harder layer on the surface. Little by little, pieces of hard rocks are separated. The layers which are below the natural 'hats' are protected and erode at a slower pace, leaving earth pillars. As the years go by, the 'hat' can crumble or the base can get thinner and thinner due to erosion by rain, and the 'hat' falls down. Then the earth pillar is bound to disintegrate quickly. That is why the Cappadocian landscape is constantly evolving.

The landscape is the glory of Cappadocia, but here is a little history.

Early History

The first signs of human habitation date from the Neolithic and the Calcolithic periods. Hearths, statuettes and tools made of volcanic glass or bone have been found. Mining and metallurgy reached its peak in Anatolia during the Early Bronze Age. Major developments were observed in northern Anatolia towards the end of this period.

Archaeological excavations discovered the first brick living quarters in Cappadocia in Asikli Höyük. Yellow and pink clay plaster was used in making the walls and floors of the houses, providing some of the most beautiful and complicated architectural examples of the first towns. They buried the dead in the Hocker position, like a foetus in the womb, in the floor of their houses.

Nowhere else in Anatolia can unique obsidian tools be found like those from Cappadocian Tumulii. Figurines, made from lightly baked clay, were unearthed together with flat stone axes wrought in many fine shapes, chisels made from bones, and ornaments made from copper, agate and other different kinds of stones. Evidence provided by a skeleton found here indicates that the earliest brain surgery known in the world was performed on a woman 20 to 25 years of age at Asikli Höyük.

The Hittites

Around 2000 BC, the Hittites, a people coming from Europe and passing through Caucasus, settled in Anatolia, where they integrated into local life. Their language was Indo-European and they were influenced by the native cultural and religious rituals. Their writing, in the shape of hieroglyphics, can be found on numerous statuettes. They progressively built an empire based in Hatusas (today's Bogazköy). After 600 years of reign they were defeated by the Phrygians and their empire was dismantled.

In the Hittite period Assyrian merchants built up trade and established centres at Kanesh Kharum and Kharum Hattush. Anatolia was rich in gold, silver and copper, but lacked tin, essential for obtaining bronze as an alloy. For this reason tin was one of the major trading materials, as well as textile goods and perfumes. The merchants had no political dominance, but were protected by the regional beys (governors).

From the 'Cappadocia tablets', cuneiform clay tablets on which ancient Assyrian was written, it has been learnt that merchants paid a 10 per cent road tax to the bey, received 30 per cent interest from locals for loans, and paid a 5 per cent tax to the Anatolian kings for goods they sold. The same tablets tell us that Assyrian merchants sometimes married Anatolian women, and the marriage agreements contained clauses to protect the women's rights from their husbands.

Assyrian merchants also introduced cylinder seals, metallurgy, their religious beliefs, gods and temples to Anatolia. Native Anatolian art flourished under the influence of Assyrian art, eventually developing its own local identity.

The Medes and Persians

A Phrygian reign was followed by the Medes (585 BC) and the Persians (547 BC). The Persians gave their people the freedom to choose their own religion and to speak their native languages. Since the religion to which they were devoted was Zoroastrian, fire was considered to be divine, and so the volcanoes of Erciyes and Hasandagi were sacred for them.

Cappadocia was left in the power of a sort of feudal aristocracy. It was included in the third Persian satrapy by Darius but was governed by rulers of its own, more or less tributary to the Great King. Later subdued by the satrap Datames, Cappadocia recovered independence under Ariarathes I, a contemporary of Alexander the Great.

The Persians constructed a 'Royal Road' connecting their capital city in Cappadocia to the Aegean region. Alexander used this road when he defeated Persian armies twice, in 334 and 332 BC, and conquered their great empire.

Greeks and Romans

After bringing the Persian Empire to an end, Alexander met with some resistance in Cappadocia. At first he tried to rule the area through one of his commanders named Sabictus, but the ruling classes and people resisted and maintained that Ariarathes I was their ruler. From 332 to 322 BC he was a successful leader, and extended the borders of the Cappadocian kingdom as far as the Black Sea.

The province was not invaded by Alexander, who contented himself with the tributary acknowledgement of his sovereignty made by Ariarathes, and the continuity of the native dynasty was only interrupted for a short time after Alexander's death, when the kingdom fell to Eumenes. His claims were made good in 322 BC by Perdiccas, who crucified Ariarathes; but in the turmoil following Eumenes's death, the son of Ariarathes recovered his inheritance and left it to a line of successors. Under the fourth of these, Cappadocia came into relations with Rome, first as an enemy of Antiochus the Great, then as an ally against Perseus of Macedon. From then on Cappadocia sided with the Roman republic against the Seleucids. Ariarathes V marched with the Roman proconsul Crassus against Aristonicus, but their forces were annihilated (130 BC). His death led to interference by the rising power of Pontus; the Cappadocians, supported by Rome against Mithridates, elected a native, Ariobarzanes, to succeed (93 BC), but it was not till Rome had given assistance that his rule was established (63 BC).

In the civil wars, Cappadocia was now for Pompey, now for Caesar, now for Antony, now against him. The Ariobarzanes dynasty came to an end and Archelaus reigned under Antony and Octavian. He maintained tributary independence until AD 17, when the Emperor Tiberius reduced Cappadocia to a province.

Cappadocia was known in Roman times for the large number of slaves who served the local rulers and who were also exported to Rome, although there they do not seem to have had a good reputation.

Vespasian in AD 70 joined Armenia Minor to it and made the combined province a frontier fortress. We still possess the report made to Hadrian by his legate Arrian, which is a valuable picture of life in a Roman frontier province in the second century.

During the reign of Emperor Septimus Severus, Cappadocia's economy flourished, but the capital, Kayseri (Caesarea), was attacked by Sassanid armies from Iran. Emperor Gordianus III ordered the construction of defensive city walls.

During this time some of the first Christians were moving from the big cities to villages. In the fourth century, when Kayseri was a flourishing religious centre, the rocky landscape of Göreme was discovered. Adopting the teachings of St Basil, Bishop of Caesarea, the Christians began to lead a monastic life in the carved-out rocks of Cappadocia.

Cappadocia remained part of the eastern empire until the eleventh century, though often invaded both by Persians and Arabs. In the eleventh century, the Turkish Seljoukides, led by their chief Alparslan, invaded Anatolia and defeated Diogenes, the Byzantine emperor. Konya became the capital of the Seljoukide State in Anatolia. Before it passed into Seljuk hands and from them to the Osmanlis, it had already become largely Armenian. The southern part was known as 'Hermeniorum terra' by the Crusaders.

35

Zelve

A strong contender for favourite place status, the Zelve monastery complex is situated about six miles from Goreme on the Avanos road. It lacks the elaborate frescoes of Goreme and other sites but there is still plenty to see.

The village was inhabited by Christians, although a small mosque at the entrance of the first valley indicates that there were a few Muslims. In 1952, the Turkish authorities moved the inhabitants to Avanos for security reasons — some walls were collapsing.

Now one can almost see the place crumbling before one's very eyes. There is probably an element of risk involved in exploring too enthusiastically, but a guide should be able to balance the thrill of stumbling through pitch black tunnels by torchlight with an element of safety.

The Zelve museum is a group of troglodyte houses and churches. In the ninth and thirteenth centuries, Zelve was an important religious city for Christians, and the major churches which can be visited are Direkli Kilise, built during the iconoclast period, in which a cross in relief can be seen; and Balikli Kilise, Üzümlü Kilise and Geyikli Kilise, built after the iconoclast period.

The churches have central naves and vaulted ceilings. Some of them contain other elements, like a dome, apses and apsidioles.

Two techniques were used to decorate the churches :
a) a technique of colour washing with no plaster or coating. Most of the time, such paintings are in red and orange.
b) a technique of fresco, which means that the rock face was previously coated with a mixture of plaster, sand and straw and was then painted with various colours.

Goreme

Many settlements in Cappadocia were established primarily as monastic communities. As Bishop of Caesarea Mazaca in the fourth century, St Basil the Great wrote the rules for monastic life that are still followed by monks and nuns of the Greek Orthodox Church. He advocated community life, prayer and physical labour, rather than the solitary asceticism which was popular at the time, and it was under his guidance that the first churches were built in Goreme Valley.

Here, a number of small communities with their own churches formed the large monastic complex. Hundreds of churches were built in this valley but none from St Basil's time remain. Most of those churches seen today were built between the seventh and thirteenth centuries, the Byzantine and Selyuk periods. At its height Goreme is said to have had a church for every day of the year. It is not just the use of the stone that is so fascinating, but the interior design. Vividly preserved during the ensuing centuries, the frescoes give us a picture of Christian belief during those times.

The only light which permeates the churches is the natural light which is filtered through the entrances. Most of the churches are quite small, and the majority are built on an inscribed cross-plan with a central cupola supported by four columns. In the north annexes of several churches are rock-cut tombs.

The most famous buildings are located inside the 'open-air museum' of Goreme. They are:

Nuns' Convent (Rahibeler), of which all that remains of any interest is the large dining hall.

St Basil's Chapel (Aziz Basil) — note its burial chambers in the floor.

The Apple Church (Elmali) is dated to the eleventh century. The yellow ochre of the region dominates the frescoes which decorate the vaulted, cross-shaped interior. As with many other Cappadocian churches, peeling paint often reveals the red as the Christian symbol of the iconoclastic period. The themes of the frescoes mainly relate to the life of Christ. As with some of the other names, 'elma' in Turkish means apple.

St Barbara's church is cut into the same rock. Like many churches it is quite small and reflects the teaching of St Basil that monastic communities should not be large in number.

Snake Church (Yilanli) may have been a funeral chapel. This eleventh-century church's fame lies not only in the quality of its frescoes, but in what they portray. The slaying of a dragon (from which the church takes its name) by St George and St Theodore on horseback, decorates the vault over the apse. Emperor Constantine (AD 306–37) and his mother Helena, holding the true cross, are depicted with the saints right next to them. The naked St Onuphrius of Egypt hides behind a palm branch.

Dark Church (Karanlik) originally only had one window, but has now been opened up to reveal some of the best eleventh-century frescoes of the adoration of the magi, the Last Supper, the betrayal by Judas and the crucifixion, as well as Christ in glory. They have retained their colour, having been in the dark for so long. *(see picture to the left)*

Shoe Church (Carikli) is named after the shoe marks on the floor. Although the narthex is in ruins, the frescoes themselves are not so damaged and mainly deal with the life of Christ. There is a portrait of the four evangelists inscribing the gospels, surrounding Christ at the centre of the dome.

Buckle Church (Tokali) is easily the loveliest of the churches, with graceful arches and beautiful frescoes. It is just outside the museum. Tokali was originally two churches, one from the tenth century and another from the eleventh century and both have some first-rate frescoes.

Nigde

Nigde was known as Nahita in the Hittite period. It lies on a plateau containing several volcanic peaks, and has always been a commercial centre, located on the trade route between Anatolia and the Mediterranean. Today is has a population of around 70,000 and is an important market town. There is a proverb, 'If there's no market at Nigde, go on to Bor', meaning 'If you go in search of something, don't give up'.

The main buildings of interest in Nigde today date from the Seljuks. The Aladdin Mosque has fine stonework over the ornate entrance, having been built in 1203 but restored in the reign of Aladdin. The fort contains an interesting clock tower. Remains from Mongol rule in the fourteenth century include the Sungur Bey Mosque and tomb, and the Hudavend Hatun Mausoleum built in 1312. The fifteenth-century Ak Medresse has been converted to an archaeological museum displaying the finds from the area, including the mummified remains of a blonde Byzantine nun of the 900s discovered in the church-filled Ihlara Valley.

The most impressive monastery in Cappadocia is the Eskigumus Monastery to the east of Nigde, off the Kayseri–Nigde road. It is the most southerly of the Cappadocian monasteries and lies close to the route taken by the invading Arabs who traversed the Taurus Mountains from the south to plunder Kayseri in the seventh century. This route follows the Tarsus River through the Cicilian Gates and was used by Alexander the Great in his eastward campaign against the Persians.

Dating mainly from the tenth century, the plain entrance to the Eskigumus Monastery was designed to hide the monastery complex from passing invaders. It was so successful that the monastery was not discovered until 1963, having escaped the vandalism to which many of the Cappadocian churches and monasteries were subjected. The large inner courtyard has high walls surrounded by monastic rooms and storage chambers. The main church is spacious and airy and its well-preserved frescoes are considered to be the best example of Byzantine art in Cappadocia.

Cappadocian Fathers

These, along with Athanaesius of Egypt, are regarded as the four key doctors of the faith in the Eastern Orthodox Church.

Basil

Basil was born in 329 at Caesarea, the capital of Cappadocia. He came from a remarkable family. His grandmother Macrina, his father Basil, and his mother Emmelia were all honoured as saints. Along with Basil, two of his brothers became bishops, and his sister a key saint of monasticism.

Basil completed his student days in Athens with a lifelong friend, Gregory of Nazianzus. When Basil returned to Caesarea he taught rhetoric for some years in the city. Then his sister persuaded him to study the monastic life. He did so, travelling to the main monastic centres of Christianity, and returned to found his own monastery on the family estate. The Rule he developed is still used in the Orthodox Church and formed the basis for that of Benedict. There are 55 items in the main Rule and a further 313 subsidiary rules in the form of questions and answers. The key change at the time was towards a communal life instead of the competition that existed among the hermits in austerity. There was an emphasis on the prayerful study of the Bible and useful work for the benefit of the whole community.

In 370 he became Archbishop of Caesarea and held the post until his death in 379. He saw one of his prime tasks as defending the Christian faith against the Arianism favoured by the emperor. At that time the Arian heresy — which denied that Christ was God in the sense of his being of the same substance with the Father — was at the height of its influence. The Emperor Valens was an Arian, and was vigorously persecuting the Catholics. St Basil's primary task as archbishop was the defence of the Catholic faith. He so overawed the Emperor Valens that he and his diocese were left alone, though there was persecution everywhere else. His answer to the Prefect Modestus may explain why. Modestus had threatened him with confiscation, exile, torture and death. St Basil said,

Well, in truth, confiscation means nothing to a man who has nothing, unless you covet these wretched rags and a few books; that is all I possess. As to exile, that means nothing to me, for I am attached to no particular place. That wherein I live is not mine, and I shall feel at home in any place to which I am sent. Or rather, I regard the whole earth as belonging to God, and I consider myself as a stranger wherever I may be. As for torture, how will you apply it? I have not a body capable of bearing it, unless you are thinking of the first blow you give me, for that will be the only one in your power. As for death, this will be a benefit to me, for it will take me the sooner to the God for whom I live . . .

The Prefect said that nobody had ever spoken to him like that. St Basil replied, 'Perhaps that is because you have never had to deal with a bishop'.

He was a model diocesan bishop. He visited every part of his diocese continually, working constantly for peace and unity in an age when controversy held sway. Basil fought simony, battled for high standards among his clergy, and denounced evil wherever he detected it. He excommunicated those involved in the widespread prostitution traffic in Cappadocia, assisted those caught up in famine, and organized a great hospital for the poor.

He died at aged forty-nine, totally worn out before he saw the fruit of his labours. As a man of learning and drive, eloquent and charitable, he was rightly esteemed as Great, and one of the key doctors of the early church.

Below are some of his more memorable sayings:

Truly unexpected news makes both ears tingle.

It is right to submit to a higher authority if in so doing a commandment of God would not be broken.

This is the definition of vice: the wrong use, in violation of the Lord's command, of what has been given us by God for a good purpose.

Christians should offer their brethren simple and unpretentious hospitality.

The indwelling of God is this — to hold God always in memory, his shrine established within us.

God chooses those who are pleasing to him. He puts a shepherd at the head of his people, and of the goat-herd Amos he made a prophet.

Good family, athletic prowess, a handsome face, tall stature, the esteem of others, control over others — none of these are important to us or fit matter for our prayers; we do not pay court to those who can boast of them. Our ideals are far higher than that.

What is the mark of a Christian? To love one another, even as Christ also loved us. To see the Lord always before him. To watch each night and day and in perfectly pleasing God to be ready, knowing that the Lord will come at an hour that he does not expect.

What is the mark of a Christian? Faith working by love. What is the mark of faith? Unhesitating conviction of the truth of the inspired words, unshaken by any argument, either based on the plea of physical necessity or masquerading in the guise of piety.

What is the mark of a believer? To hold fast by such conviction in the strength of what Scripture says and to dare neither to set it at naught nor to add to it.

Despise the flesh, for it passes away; be solicitous for your spirit, for it will never die.

Gregory of Nazianzus

Gregory was born at Arianazus, near Nazianzus, about AD 330. He was the son of Gregory, Bishop of Nazianzus. His mother, Nonna, proved very influential in his spiritual life.

He was educated in Caesarea (Cappadocia), Alexandria and Athens, and while there, with his friend Basil he compiled a book of Origen's writings.

Although Arianism had been condemned at the Council of Nicea in 325, several emperors after Constantine favoured this heresy, mainly because it was adopted by the Goths who were the core of the army. Gregory returned home in 359 to help his father counter the Arians. At that time, with his friend Basil, he took up the monastic life.

In 372 Basil, now Archbishop, made him Bishop of Sasima. Gregory regarded it as a detestable place without water or food, and continued to live at Nazianzus.

In 379 Gregory was asked to go to Constantinople. It was there that he preached five sermons on the Trinity. For thirty years Arianism had held sway with the support of the emperor, but people accepted Gregory's teaching and in 381 he was made Bishop of Constantinople and hosted the Council of Constantinople that year.

During the Council he asked to retire, and left the world of ecclesiastical politics, writing: 'My mind is, if I must write the truth, to keep clear of every conference of bishops, for of conference I never saw good come, or a remedy so much as an increase of evils. For there is strife and ambition, and those have the upper hand of reason'. However the Council did ratify the Nicean Creed and condemn Apollinarianism which seemed to deny the full humanity of Christ, before 'politics' took over with ecclesiastical appointments!

Gregory returned to his estate near Nazianzus, where he died in 389, his work in defending the person of Christ accomplished.

> We do not separate the Man from the Deity, no, we assert the dogma of the unity and identity of the Person, who in past times was not man but God, the only Son before all ages, who in these last days has assumed manhood also for our salvation; in his flesh passible, in his deity impassible; in the body circumscribed, uncircumscribed in the Spirit; at once earthly and heavenly, tangible and intangible, comprehensible and incomprehensible; that by one and the same person, perfect man and perfect God, the whole humanity, fallen through sin, might be created anew.

An easier quotation to remember is:

Christ is born: glorify him.
Christ comes from heaven: go out to meet him.
Christ descends to earth: let us be raised on high.

Gregory of Nyssa

Gregory's date of birth, as that of his death, is unknown, but it is thought that he was born around AD 333 and died around 390.

We do know that he was a younger brother of Basil, who seems to have had considerable control or influence on his life. Along with his brother, he was educated in Athens and became interested in the works of Origen. Around this time he married Theosebeia. He seems to have become dissatisfied with the secular world of rhetoric and wrote, 'Secular education is truly barren. It is always in labour and never brings anything to birth'.

On his return from Athens he adopted the life of a priest and hermit. We are not sure what happened to his wife at this time, but he seems to have stayed with her until her death.

Basil consecrated him and made him Bishop of Nyssa (between Caesarea and Ankara) in 372. He was basically a theologian, and proved so hopeless at administration that he was unable to account for the church property and at one point was arrested by the Governor of Pontus on the assumption that he had stolen it.

After Basil's death in 379, Gregory was able to employ his rhetorical and theological ability and was a major influence at the Council of Antioch that year and at the Council of Constantinople in 381. There on several occasions he was called upon to give major addresses at enthronements or state funerals.

Most of his writing was against false teaching, although there are some works, like one on virginity, which were highly valued within monastic circles. Below are some of his more memorable sayings:

> Cling only to what is necessary.

> He who give you the day will also give you the things necessary for the day.

> Just as those lost at sea regain their right course by the light of some beacon or mountain peak, so the Scripture guides those adrift on the sea of life to the harbour of God's will.

Antioch in Pisidia

As with other Antiochs, the town began in the fourth century BC when Seleucus named it after his father. Like Rome it was built on seven hills. It is located on the right bank of the river Anthius, about 1,100 metres above sea level and close to the modern town of Yalvac (population 30,000).

Before Seleucus founded the Greek town, the site may have been used for the worship of the Phrygian god Men. It was made a free city by the Romans in 189 BC. By 11 BC Augustus had given it the status of a Roman colony and named it Caesaria. It became the centre of civil and military administration in south Galatia. By the time Paul arrived in the reign of Claudius (AD 41–54) it was a prosperous Roman city at a junction on the Via Sebaste linking Ephesus to Syria. It was abandoned after Arab attacks in the eighth century. In 1097 there was enough remaining for the Crusaders to find it a useful place for refuge on their journey to the east.

When Seleucus founded Antioch he brought in a mixed group of settlers Phrygians from the nearby area, as well as Greeks and Jews. Later, around 200 BC, two thousand Jewish families were brought in from Babylon. Augustus and others brought in veterans from the Roman army who retained their loyalty to Rome far longer than in many other cities in the region. When Paul arrived he found that a large number of diaspora Jews, who had adapted to the local culture, had become rich, and among them some were Roman citizens. They certainly had enough power to make sure that even Paul, a Roman citizen, could be banished from their town.

Latin seems to have been well used in the town, and a fragment of the Res Gestae of Augustus has been found, along with many other Latin inscriptions. Greek and the local Phrygian language would also have been in regular use. It is likely that Paul used Greek here, as he did throughout his travels.

Paul at Antioch in Pisidia

The sermon preached by Paul at Antioch (Acts 13) is obviously regarded by Luke as a model sermon indicating Paul's approach to the diaspora Jews and their proselytes. There is an excellent commentary on this by David Gooding in *True to the Faith* (Hodder & Stoughton, 1990) pp.211–22.

There are similarities with Stephen's speech before the Sanhedrin in Acts 7 and with Peter's sermons. As with those sermons, we find the key facts that Jesus died, was buried, was raised and appeared to many. So we have the key gospel events, backed up by the witness of the Old Testament and those who knew Jesus in the flesh, the great gospel promises of salvation through Christ and new life in the Spirit, and the gospel conditions of repentance and faith.

Paul opens his sermon, in which he sets out to prove that Jesus is the Saviour, by concentrating on a key issue in Jewish life — the provision of the land. It is still the key issue for Jews today. Then from verse 26 he turns to Jesus as the fulfilment of all God's promises before concluding with the challenge to accept Jesus.

> Paul is impressive because he can not only articulate the historical facts clearly but he can interpret their significance and apply it both corporately and personally. This remarkable ability, seen supremely in Jesus, was absent in most of the teachers of the law who knew the minutiae of the scriptures but not what their purpose was.
> (S. Gaukroger, *Acts*, Crossway Bible Guide [Leicester: Crossway Books 1993] p.114.)

> In Acts 13 Paul is addressing Galatians. Only a few months or so later he will be writing his Letter to the Galatians. It is very striking, therefore, that he brings together here at the conclusion of his sermon five of the great words that will be foundation stones of his gospel as he expounds it in his letter. Having referred to Jesus' death on the tree (v.29), he goes on to speak of sin (v.38), faith, justification, law (v.39) and grace (v.43).
> (J.R.W.Stott, *Message of Acts*, Bible Speaks Today [Leicester: IVP, 1990] p.225.)

Antioch in Pisidia today

A visit to Yalvac museum, near the town centre, is well worth the time spent. It has a useful plan of the ruins and a reconstruction of a wealthy home from the Ottoman era.

Pisidian Antioch is entered through the City gate. It was built in AD 129 when the Emperor Hadrian visited the area. The gate is decorated with weapons and garlands symbolizing the military power of Rome. Leading up the hill from the gate is a wide road. In the centre was a two-metre wide waterfall dropping down through a series of steps, and on each side of the road there were shops.

The roadway turns right up the Decumanus Maximus to the Theatre. Much of the stonework has been removed but recent excavation has revealed the stage area. The theatre was enlarged in AD 312 by building over the Decumanus Maximus, which passed under the seating in a tunnel 5 metres high and 55 metres long. At full capacity the theatre held around 12,000 and so was roughly the same capacity as that at Aspendos.

Turning left at the top of the street we reach the Church of St Bassus of Antioch. The building dates from the fifth century. From the church we can look up the hill across the Tiberius Square to the Temple of Augustus. The square contained shops and places for eating and drinking. Sadly most of the stonework has been used, even as late as 1970, by the people of Yalvac.

All that remains of the Propylon are twelve steps at the end of the square. It was built in 2 BC in honour of Augustus. The finely decorated triple arch was about 15 metres wide and 10 metres high. Climbing up the remains of the stairs reveals an area of 100 metres by 85 metres surrounded by porticoes with the temple of Augustus in the centre. The whole structure surpassed any other in the region.

The Nympheum is reached by retracing our visit to the Cardo Maximus and walking 300 metres to the north. The reservoir was 27 metres by 3 metres and fed a pool twice that area. In turn it was fed from an eleven-kilometre long aquaduct bringing water from the Sultan mountains. The remains of the aquaduct can be best seen from the baths.

The bathhouse complex to the west measures 70 metres by 55 metres and seems to have been constructed around the time of the nympheum before AD 50. This means that the key buildings of Pisidian Antioch were there at the time of Paul's visit. It makes the site almost unique, as in most other places the buildings date from a time after Paul.

The great church of St Paul is in the south-east corner of the site. It was the earliest of the basilicas found in Anatolia and dates from around AD 370, although alterations were made at a later date. The church held a large number of worshippers and measures 70 metres by 27 metres. An inscription identifies it as dedicated to St Paul and it seems to have been built over a synagogue. So this could have been the site at which Paul preached the sermon recorded in Acts 13.

H. V. Morton, in *The Steps of St Paul* (1936), makes the following observation:

> The more I explored the ruined cities of Asia Minor, the more truly I realised that the history of man in this country was writ literally in water...

> Travelling across a burning plain, I have come to a mound covered with little stones which whiten the ground for miles. I pick one up and see that it is a chip of marble that had come long ago in a ship from Greece; another stone is red, a chip of porphyry from Egypt. They are the only signs that centuries ago philosophers argued beneath the columns of the market place, that sculptors strove to create beauty there, that merchants unloaded spices, perfumes, and gold for the adornment of fastidious painted women.

> How is it possible that such desolate clefts in the hills and such cruel deserts could have supported the life of the classical world? The answer is, of course, water. It may not be visible there today. The stream may have dried up, or it may be running to waste on the wrong side of the hill. But wherever you encounter a ruin in an inhospitable and uninhabited part of Asia Minor, you may be sure that the Greeks or

the Romans had once built an aqueduct that bore a sparkling stream from a neighbouring mountain into the heart of the city...

A civilization built on aqueducts is a perilous one. Unless you are strong enough to defend your life-giving archway, one barbarian with a pickaxe can turn your city into a parched desert. Once the aqueduct is broken, the life of the city is ended. Asphodels will grow in the cracks of the agora, the roofs will fall, crushing the marble shelves of libraries, birds will nest in the dry cups of the public fountains, and the jackal will nurse her young in the temple court.

And this has happened to the shining cities of the Hellenistic Age. The barbarians allowed the water to spill itself into the earth. They pitched their tents near the break in the aqueduct so that they could scoop up the water in their hands. So century by century the walls of the cities have fallen. The marble streets have been rent asunder to provide stones for sheepfolds. Shining pillars, brought in ships from Greece and from Egypt, have been pulled down to be inserted horizontally into walls. Graves have been rifled for hidden gold and for marble coffins: the carved sarcophagus, in which a Roman was laid to rest, makes, after all, a perfect drinking-trough for goats.

Therefore, in the broken aqueduct of Pisidian Antioch you can read the tragic history of the downfall of the proud cities of Asia Minor, which in ancient times shone among the great names of the world.

Iconium

Iconium, now known as Konya, is at an altitude of just over 1,000 metres on the south-west edge of the Anatolian plateau. It is the centre of a fertile plain. To the west is the Bozkir mountain and to the south the Taurus range. The old city is to the east of the acropolis.

Today it is the fourth or fifth largest city in Turkey with a population in excess of 600,000.

Two legends are told about its name. The first relates how Perseus killed a dragon, and the people set up a monument with his icon in his honour: hence Iconium. Muslims tell of two dervishes flying towards the west. One asked 'Shall I land?'; the other replied 'Yes, land' (Kon ya)!

The Phrygians claimed that it was the first city to be established after the great flood of Noah.

What we do know is that excavations in the area show settlements going back to the late stone age (7000 BC), followed by habitation in the Calcolitic, Bronze, Hittite, Lydian, Persian and Greco-Roman times.

The Hittites called it Kuwanna and the Phygians Kowania, which is getting close to its later name of Iconium. After the conquest of Alexander it came under Seleucid rule, and although it was transferred to Pergamum in 190 BC it never seems to have been under their control. It became a self-governing city, strongly Greek in language and culture. Various rulers claimed it until, in 25 BC, it became part of the Roman province of Galatia. Cicero and others regarded it as part of Lycaonia, but those who visited the city, like Xenophon and Pliny, describe it as being in Phrygia, as Luke states in his account of Paul's visit.

Claudius honoured it by renaming the city with his name! Hadrian (AD 130) made it a colony, and from then on it seems to have been retained as the leading city in the area, as it is to this day. It has always been a centre for commerce, on the trade route to the east, rather than for defence, and so frequently changed hands. Little remains of the Graeco-Roman period.

Christian Iconium

Iconium is known for the visits of St Paul in Acts 14 and 16 and in the early church for the 'Acts of Paul and Thecla'. The story runs like this. Thecla of Iconium is impressed by Paul's teaching and refuses to marry her fiancé. He makes a complaint and she is condemned by the proconsul to be burnt, while Paul is to be whipped. But rain puts out the fire, and, having gained her freedom, she once more seeks out Paul and follows him when he returns to Antioch. Here again she refuses an offer of marriage and once more is condemned, this time in the arena. There a lioness protects her. In the greatest of danger she baptizes herself by jumping into a moat. She encounters other serious dangers but in the end is set free. She puts on men's clothes and once more follows Paul. She dies in her old age at Seleucia.

A council was held at Iconium in 232. Later, Eusebius mentions that Celcus, Bishop of Iconium in the mid 200s, permitted a layman Paulinus to do church work and that Nikomas was bishop in the 260s. Numerous inscriptions and frescoes dating from the third century have been found around Iconium, which seems to have been an early centre for the faith.

Islamic Konya

Konya's main claim to fame today is that it was the city of Mevlana Rumi, who moved to Konya in 1240 from the east. In 1244 a mystic, Shams al-Din, came to Konya and had a transforming effect on Rumi's life. Rumi began composing vast tomes of poetry, but he is best known for the community he established.

The Sema, with its distinctive whirling dance displays, in seven parts, is the mystical journey of a follower's ascent through mind and love to the divine. The Sufi dervish turns towards truth, grows through love, abandons himself, and embraces perfection. He is dressed in a long white gown, symbolizing the burial shroud, while the cone-shaped hat symbolizes the tombstone of self. The right hand held high receives blessings from God, and the left hand held low conveys these to the earth. The tomb of Rumi is now in the Mevlana museum and is an important Islamic shrine. The dances put on for tourists today are performed by professional dancers rather than devotees of Rumi.

Lystra

Lystra is located about 18 miles to the south of Iconium. The site, just north of Hatunsaray, was confirmed by J. R. Sterrett in 1885 and has not been disputed. It is in a valley just before the hills begin to rise towards the Taurus mountains at the junction of two small rivers. It is 1,200 metres above sea level and over 100 metres higher than Iconium. The tell is on the left down a minor road sign-posted just before the bridge entering Hatunsaray. It is best climbed by crossing a small field and walking to the left of the mound. The climb is relatively easy from this point which seems to follow the route between the city and the temple of Zeus on which the people took Paul and Barnabas.

It may have been inhabited for many centuries but little is known until Roman times. In AD 6 Augustus designated Lystra as a Roman colony to serve as a defense against the bandits who lived in the Taurus mountains to the south. Lystra was connected to Iconium and Derbe by a main road. It seems to have retained its strong local Lycaonian customs and language, with Latin used for inscriptions and public notices. It was not proven to be a Roman colony until 1885 when Waddington found a coin with the Latin inscription COLONIA . IULIA . FELIX . GEMINA . LUSTRA (the Latin form Lustra, instead of the Greek Lystra, is usual on coins and inscriptions). The people of Lystra sent a statue of Concord to Pisidian Antioch towards the end of the second century as a sign of their loyalty to the main Roman garrison.

The remains of Lystra are considerable for such a small place. The central area was fortified, but the town extended over the lower ground to the east and south. A large basin bearing an inscription in honour of Augustus stands probably in its original position, and perhaps indicates the site of a sacred place, *Augusteum,* dedicated to the worship of the Emperor and of Rome. This could well have been the site for the worship of Zeus, as the two were often linked. There would have been a college of priests attached to the temple, which would have had the description Propoleos, as in the 'Western text', as the temple stood outside the city. The sacrifice to Paul and Barnabas, in celebration of the epiphany of the gods, was probably made at the entrance to the sacred precinct.

Paul at Lystra

Acts 14:8–20 gives us the description of the lame man at Lystra, and of his healing. It is similar to that of the lame man in the temple court at Jerusalem (Acts 3). In each case, faith in Jesus is the key to healing. What followed is unique to Lystra and is full of local features.

The bystanders were not the few Roman citizens of the colony, whose language (as appears from funerary inscriptions) was Latin, but the local Lycaonians who used their own language. Paul and Barnabas realized that it was not the same as languages they had encountered elsewhere. So they did not grasp what was happening until the preparations for the sacrifices were well advanced.

The people assumed that such a miracle could only be performed by a visit from a god. Local legend told of earlier occasions when the gods had come down to them in the likeness of men, in particular, the two gods whom the Greeks knew as Zeus and Hermes. Ovid tells the story of an aged and pious couple of that region, Philemon and Baucis by name, who entertained Jupiter and Mercury (the Roman equivalents of Zeus and Hermes) unawares, and were rewarded for their hospitality. We also know from local inscriptions, like those found at nearby Sedasa, that the worship of Zeus and Hermes was linked. One dating from the middle of the third century, and discovered by Professor W. M. Calder, records the dedication to Zeus of a statue of Hermes by men with Lycaonian names. Zeus was the chief god in the Greek pantheon; Hermes, son of Zeus by Maia, was the herald of the gods. Barnabas may have been identified with Zeus because of his more dignified bearing; Paul, the more animated of the two, was called Hermes. Iamblichus describes Hermes as the god who is foremost in speaking. So in their religion it was considered right and proper that the people were prepared to sacrifice to these gods who had appeared in human form.

Paul now speaks to the local pagan people in a similar way to which he spoke to those at Athens and elsewhere: see I Thessalonians 1:9. To Jews, who already know that God is one, and that he is the living and true God. Paul proclaims that Jesus is the Christ. Pagans must first be taught what Jews already believe: that God is one and that he has left sure evidence of this for all to see.

Derbe

There are few mentions of Derbe in earlier years. Its name may have come from the Lycaonian *delbeia,* which means juniper. We know that around the time of the Roman conquest the ruler was Anitpater the pirate, and that probably refers to the large numbers of robbers who were in the area. Antipater was not totally bad, and had welcomed Cicero when he was governor of Cilicia.

The Romans made Derbe one of their colonies in an attempt to bring law and order as well as to collect customs duties, as it was a frontier city on the road to the East. Derbe, like Lystra, was in the administrative area of Lycaonia (Acts 14:6). It had also, like Iconium, been given a new name by Claudius — Claudioderbe!

At the turn of the twentieth century J. R. Sterrett and W. M. Ramsey maintained that the mound of Gudelisin was the site of Derbe. They based this theory primarily on the distance from Lystra being about a day's journey away. However, recently discovered evidence, in the form of two inscriptions, has fairly positively identified the mound of Kerti Hiiyiik as the site of Derbe. It is a sizable mound signposted about 15 miles north-east of Karaman (ancient Laranda). This would make it at least two days' journey from Lystra and would have given Paul and Barnabas a safe haven some distance from their opponents in Lystra and Iconium.

The first inscription was discovered at Kerti Hiiyiik in 1956 by Michael Ballance. It is a dedication by the council and people of Derbe and can be dated in AD 157. The inscription is now in the courtyard of the Archaeological Museum in Konya. It is placed alongside inscriptions relating to Iconium and Lystra on the left of the entrance to the main hall of the museum.

The second inscription was discovered in 1962 in the village of Suduraya, having been brought there from Kerti Hiiyiik, and comes from the end of the fourth century. The inscription is on the tombstone of a Bishop of Derbe named Michael.

The site awaits further excavation, but the location does explain why Paul waited until the next morning to set out for a place that was some distance away (Acts 14:20).

The second inscription also provides further evidence of the Christian church at Derbe. We know the names of five bishops, one of whom, Daphnus, was present at the Council of Constantinople in AD 381.

Luke reports that after preaching the gospel in Derbe and making many disciples in that city, Paul returned to Lystra (Acts 14:20f.). Maybe friends had come from Lystra to let them know that it would be safe to return — other matters were filling the headlines!

Paul revisited Derbe on his second missionary journey (16:1) and it is possible that he also passed through Derbe at the beginning of his third missionary journey (18:23). Gaius, a disciple and companion of Paul from Derbe, is mentioned in Acts 20:4.

The site of Derbe is in an area known as that of the 1001 churches, including the monastery at Alahan. This area was 'discovered' by Sir William Ramsey at the turn of the twentieth century. In the village of Madensehir there are at least three churches and two large sarcophagi. Then high up the valley is another village that seems to be packed with church ruins. The dirt road there is not for those who dislike heights. Also within a day's walk is the monastery of the Archangel Michael at Mount Karadag (now in a military zone.). The main occupation of these hidden churches seems to have been in the time of the Arab and then of the Seljuk invasions. Christians found the isolated, inaccessible area an ideal place to hide and the large number of churches may reflect the number of villages from which the Christians fled. The combination of steep cliffs, wooded hillsides, and being well away from the road system, allowed the Christian community to continue in peace for many years. So from our knowledge of its bishop and nearby buildings, it appears that Paul's initial work in this area bore much fruit for years to come.

Antalya

The area has been inhabited for many thousands of years. In the Karain Cave, near Yagcikoy, 16 miles north-west of Antalya, remains of the Paleolithic, Mesolithic, Neolithic, Chalcolithic and Bronze Ages were unearthed.

The Hittites ruled Antalya from 2500–1400 BC. Tribes from Trakya during the eighth century BC put an end to their rule, and the city states of Pamphylia, Lycia and Cicilia were founded. Today's province of Antalya entirely covers Pamphylia.

The word Pamphylia is of Greek origin and is composed of *pan*, meaning many, and *phyla,* meaning race. It reflects the make-up of the population of the area.

From the seventh century to the year 546 BC, Antalya was under the sovereignty of the Lydians, when it was replaced by that of the Persians. The Macedonian commander Alexander the Great put an end to their rule in 336 BC, when he conquered all the cities of the region (with the exception of one or two places like Termessos). When Alexander died in 323 BC, a war, which was to last for several years, started between his generals and continued with various conflicts until 188 BC. The King of Pergamum made good use of these conflicts to extend his own territory to include Antalya. Attalos II (159–138 BC) of Pergamum rebuilt the existing city, and the one we know today as Antalya came into being. From that time on it has been known successively as Attaleis, Adalia, Adalya and finally Antalya.

In AD 43 Claudius formed a kingdom uniting Pamphylia and Lycia. It was at this time that Paul and Barnabas sailed back to Antioch from Attalia (Acts 14:25–6). In the second and third centuries AD, Antalya lived its most prosperous period. During the second century, Christianity began to spread in the region, while under the sovereignty of Byzantium, and up to the fifth and sixth centuries AD, Antalya is known to have experienced another phase of development. During these centuries the city overflowed beyond its walls.

In the seventh century AD the influence of Moslem Arabs began to make itself felt. In 860 AD Admiral Fazl took Antalya. It fell again to the Byzantium emperors, was taken by Suleiman in 1085, and taken again by Emperor Alexius in 1103. In all it changed hands at least six times. It seems to have finally come under Ottoman rule in 1391 in the time of Murat I. After the First World War it was held for three years by the Italians.

An evening stroll

The ancient city centre is called the Kale Ici. The narrow streets run from the harbour and along by the walls. The difference in the houses shows the economic status of the owners or the purpose for which they were used. However, they share many common factors. Most of them were built of stone and timber.

Each one has a front and back garden. There are very few windows on the street side of the first floor of the house. On the top floor is a cumba — a projection adorned with wooden ornaments. The centre of the house is on the ground floor and opens onto a paved courtyard called a taslik where there are wooden benches. This leads into the ground floor rooms and there is also a staircase to the upper floors. The ground floor is largely the house's servicing area and consists of the kitchen, storage room, etc., while the upper floor contains the living quarters, although a kitchen and a storage room can sometimes be seen on the top floor. The upper floor rooms are larger and lighter, with large windows. In some of these houses the top floor rooms have two rows of windows, one on top of the other; and in some cases the upper rows do not have any glass, only wooden lattices. The bottom row can be opened. In the upper part of some of the cumba are small pieces of glass, sometimes coloured. A few of the buildings near the harbour have been restored. Today the area is bustling with restaurants, shops selling souvenirs and old carpets, as well as supplies for the yachts.

Hadrian's Gate was built in AD 130 in honour of the emperor. It is considered as Pamphylia's finest gate. The upper part has three apertures in the shape of a cupola, and except for the pillars is built entirely of white marble with striking ornamentation. The original gate held two storeys but no trace is left of the top storey.

Perge

Perge, one of Pamphylia's (land of many tribes) foremost cities, was founded on a wide plain between two hills three miles west of the Kestros (Aksu) river.   We read of Paul, Barnabas and Mark arriving there from Cyprus (Acts 13:13). On their return journey, after preaching in Perge (14:25), they left from Attalia which even by Paul's time was the major port. Perge seems to have been just accessible to small ships, and being far enough away from the sea it escaped attacks by pirates.

There does seem to have been a Hittite settlement around 1500 BC named Parha. However, Strabo claims that the city was founded after the Trojan War (around 1100 BC) by colonists from Argos under the leadership of heroes named Mopsos and Calchas. Statue bases at the city gate, dating from around AD 120, mention the names of seven legendary founders: Mopsos, Calchas, Riksos, Labos, Machaon, Leonteus and Minyasas.

Perge was under Lydian, and then Persian, rule until the arrival of Alexander the Great, when in 333 BC it surrendered to Alexander without resistance.   At the time it had no protective walls. With the death of Alexander, Perge was soon lost by Antigonus to the Seleucids. After the treaty of Apamea, the Roman consul Manlius Vulso was sent from Rome in 188 BC to regain the town for Pergamum. So Perge passed to Pergamum and a road was constructed to link the two places.

In 133 BC, when the kingdom of Pergamum was turned over to Rome, it came under Roman rule. In 79 BC Cicero accused the Roman administrator Gaius Verres, before the Senate, of unlawful conduct in Perge, saying, 'As you know, there is a very old and sacred temple to Diana in Perge. I assert that this was also robbed and looted by Verres and that the gold was stripped from the statue of Diana and stolen'. No trace of this temple has been found. Artemis was portrayed on local coins under her Pamphylian name of Vanassa Preiia. Her form has also been found on many statues from Perga.

Over the first three centuries AD, Perge became one of the finest cities in whole region of Anatolia. There was a considerable Roman presence — a third of the names on inscriptions are Roman.

Perge became an important centre of Christianity. Nestor and Tribimius were martyred in the Decian persecution of AD 251. The Notiti Episcopatuum mentions the city as metropolis of Pamphylia Secunda until the thirteenth century. We know of 11 bishops: Epidaurus, present at the Council of Ancyra (312); Callicles at Nicæa (325); Berenianus at Constantinople (426); Epiphanius at Ephesus (449), and at Chalcedon (451); Hilarianus, at the Council of Constantinople (536); Eulogius at Constantinople (553); Apergius, condemned as a Monothelite, at Constantinople (680); John at the Trullan Council (692); Sisinnius Pastillas (about 754); an Iconoclast, condemned at Nicæa (787); Constans at Nicæa (787); and John at Constantinople (869). St Matrona of Perge, about AD 500, was an abbess in Constantinople and noted for the fact that she wore men's clothes and had been married and given birth to a daughter.

After the Arab raids of the mid-seventh century, the residents and their bishop moved to Antalya. There may have been a small village until the thirteenth century, but from then we hear no more until the coming of the 'archaeologists' in the 1800s.

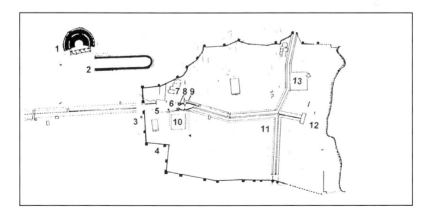

Plan of Perge – numbers as in text of visit

Perge — a visit

The theatre (1) is on the southern slopes of Mt Kocabele. The cavea, slightly more than a semicircle, is divided in two by a wide diazoma. It contains 19 seat levels below, and 23 above, giving around 13,000 seats. Spectators reached the diazoma from the parados on either side via vaulted passages and stairs. The orchestra, situated between the cavea and the stage building, is wider than a semicircle. It may have been used as an arena in the third century, as there is evidence of carved balustrade panels which passed between marble knobs.

The partially standing two-storey stage building can be dated to the middle of the second century AD. On the facade, columns between the five doors support a narrow podium above. The theatre's most striking feature is a series of marble reliefs of mythological subjects decorating the face of this podium. The first relief on the right portrays the local god personifying the Kestros (Aksu) river, Perge's lifeblood, along with a nymph. From here on, the reliefs depict the entire life story of Dionysos, the god of wine and the founder and protector of theatres. Dionysos was the son of Zeus and Semele, who was reputed to be as beautiful as Spring. Hera, his wife, ever jealous of her husband, wanted to get rid of Semele, along with her son. She begged Semele to persuade Zeus to let her see him in all his might and glory. The credulous Semele was taken in by the ruse and implored Zeus to acquiesce. Zeus, unable to resist the pleas of his beloved, came down from Olympos on his golden chariot and appeared before her, but the mortal Semele could not withstand his radiance and was consumed by fire. Dying, she gave birth to the fruit of her love, who had not yet come to full term, and threw him from the flames. Zeus took this little boy, sewed him into his hip and kept him there until his term was completed. It is in this way that the boy was given the name Dionysos — born once from his mother's womb and coming into the world a second time from his father's hip (panel 2). So that the infant could be protected from Hera's malevolence, fed and brought to manhood, he was taken by Hermes to the nymphs of Mount Nysa, who raised the boy in a cave, giving him love and careful attention (panel 3). Finally, as a young man, Dionysos one day drank the juice of all the grapes on the vine growing along the cave's walls. This is how wine was discovered. With the aim of introducing his new drink into every corner of the globe and spreading the knowledge of viniculture, the god of wine went on a journey around the world in a chariot drawn by two panthers.

Another scene from a five metre-long frieze shows Tyche holding a cornucopia in her left hand, and in her right a cult statue. On either side are the figures of an old man and two youths bringing bulls for sacrifice to the goddess.

The Stadium (2) is one of the best preserved from the ancient world. It measures 34 x 334 metres, with the opening at its south end. It is very likely that the building was entered at this point via a monumental wooden door. The stadium was built on a substructure of 70 vaulted chambers, 30 along each side and 10 on its narrow northern end. These chambers are interconnected, with every third compartment providing entrance to the theatre. From inscriptions over the remaining compartments, giving the names of their owners and listing various types of goods, it is clear that these spaces were used as shops. The tiers of seats which lie on top of these vaulted rooms, provided a seating capacity of 12,000. The stadium was built for holding five games: sprint running, the marathon, boxing, wrestling and the pentathlon. When gladiatorial and wild-animal combat became popular in the mid-third century, the north end of the stadium was surrounded with a protective balustrade and turned into an arena. Its architectural style and stone work date from the second century AD.

The Tomb of Plancia Magna (3) is that of the daughter of Plancius Verus, the Governor of Bithynia. She was a wealthy and civic-minded woman, and because of her community service, the people, assembly and senate erected statues of her. She seems to have been a demiurgos, which was the highest civil servant in the city's government, as well as a priestess of Artemis Pergaia and the head priestess of the cult of the emperor.

A large part of Perge is encircled by walls (4) which in some places go back to the Hellenistic period, but most date from the fourth century AD when invasions threatened. On entering the city there is a small rectangular court 40 metres long, bounded by walls of later date. From this courtyard one continues through a second, southern gate built in the form of a triumphal arch (5) and highly decorated, particularly on the back. This gate leads into a trapezoidal courtyard 92 metres long and 46 metres wide. On the west wall of this court, which was used as a ceremonial site during the reign of Emperor Septimius Severus (AD 193–211) is a monumental fountain or nymphaeum (6). The building consists of a wide pool, and behind it a two-storeyed richly worked facade. It was dedicated to Artemis Pergaia, Septimius Severus and his wife Julia Domna, and their sons.

A monumental propylon directly north of the nymphaeum opens onto the largest and most magnificent bath in Pamphylia (7). A large pool (natacia) measuring 13 x 20 metres covers the inside of an apsed chamber on the south portico of a broad palaestra; the palaestra is bounded in front by a portico. Pergaians cleansed themselves in this pool after exercising in the palaestra. This area was very grand, with a facade, coloured marble facing, and the statues of Genius, Heracles, Hygiea, Asklepios and Nemesis. From here another door leads to the frigidarium, a space which also contained a pool. Before entering, bathers washed their feet in water flowing along a shallow channel running the full length of the pool's north side. The frigidarium was adorned with statues of the Muses. Next are the tepidarium and the caldarium, which connect with each other. Beneath these rooms are bricks belonging to the hypocaust system which circulated the hot air coming from the boiler room. In the Roman era the bath was not just a place for washing, but was also a place where men met to pass the time of day or to discuss a variety of important topics. The long rectangular compartment at the north of the frigidarium was probably a place where bathers strolled and chatted. A long marble bench extends along this room's west wall. Inscriptions on a large number of plinths found during excavations, indicate that the statues which once stood on them were donated by a man named Claudius Peison.

At the northern end of the inner court is a Hellenistic gate (8), which is Perge's most magnificent structure. It consisted of two towers with a horseshoe-shaped court behind them. The towers had three storeys and were covered with a conical roof. With the aid of Plancia Magna, several alterations in the decoration of the court were made between AD 120 and 122 changing it from a defensive structure to a court of honour. To create a facade, the Hellenistic walls were covered with slabs of coloured marble, several new niches were opened, and Corinthian columns were added. Figures of gods and goddesses like Aphrodite, Hermes, Pan and the Dioskouroi occupied the niches on the lower level. Inscribed bases of nine statues have been found, but the statues themselves have not been recovered. According to their inscriptions, these statues, which must have been placed in the niches on the upper level, represent the legendary heroes who founded Perge after the Trojan Wars. In inscriptions on two pedestals, the names M. Plancius Varus and C. Plancius Varus, his son, appear with the adjective meaning 'founder'. Essentially because of their goodness and generosity toward Perge, they were accepted as second founders for whom this honour seemed appropriate.

To the north of the court is a three-arched monumental arch (9) built by Plancia Magna. Inscriptions on pedestals unearthed in excavations indicate that statues of the emperors and their wives, from the reign of Nerva to Hadrian, stood in the niches.

An agora (10) 65 metres square is located to the east of the Hellenistic gate. On all sides it is surrounded by a wide stoa with shops. In the centre may be the remains of a temple to the goddess Tyche or Fortuna. The floor of these shops is paved with coloured mosaics. An interesting stone used in an ancient game can be seen in front of one store in the north portico. The game, which was played with six stones per person and thrown like dice, must have been very popular throughout the region, as similar stones were also found in other neighbouring cities.

A colonnaded street (11) runs north–south through the city centre — going under the triumphal arch of Demetrios-Apollonios at a point near the acropolis. This thoroughfare is intersected by another running east–west. On both sides of this 250 metre-long street are broad porticoes behind which are rows of shops. In this way the columned architecture on both sides offers various examples of the Roman understanding of perspective. The porticoes also provided a place where people could both take shelter from the violent rains in winter and protect themselves from Perge's extremely hot summer sun. Because of their suitability for the climate, avenues of this type are frequently found in the cities of southern and western Anatolia. Certainly the most interesting aspect of Perge's colonnaded street is the pool-like water channel which divides the road down the middle. Thought to be made to flow by the river god Kestros, these cooling waters ran out of a nymphaeum at the north end of the street.

At approximately the middle of the street, four relief-carved columns belonging to the portico immediately catch the eye. On the first column, Apollo is depicted riding a chariot drawn by four horses; on the second is Artemis the huntress; the third shows Calchas, one of the city's mythical founders; and the last, Tyche (Fortune).

The main road comes to an end at another nymphaeum (12) built at the foot of the acropolis in the second century AD. The rich architecture of its two-tiered facade and its numerous statues make it one of Perge's most striking monuments. The water brought from the spring empties into a pool beneath the statue of the river god Kestros — which stands precisely in the centre of the fountain — and from there flows to the streets via channels.

The Palaestra (13), Perge's oldest building, is reached by turning left from the triumphal arch of Apollonios which intersects the streets, and passing the Hellenistic gate. Here the youth of the city practised wrestling and underwent physical education. According to an inscription, this square edifice, consisting of an open area surrounded by rooms, was dedicated to the Emperor Claudius (AD 41–54) by Julius Cornutus.

Among the famous men raised in this city can be cited the physician Asklepiades, the sophist Varus, and the mathematician Apollonios, who first analysed and set out the properties of conic sections (second century BC).

Aspendos

Aspendos was founded by colonists from Argos in the seventh century BC, although they probably took over an earlier settlement. A late eighth-century BC bilingual inscription, carved in both Hittite hieroglyphs and the Phoenician alphabet and discovered in the 1947 excavation of Karatepe near Adana, states that Asitawada, the king of Danunum (Adana), founded a city called Azitawadda, a derivation of his own name, and that he was a member of the Muksas, or Mopsus, dynasty. The striking similarity between the names 'Estwediiys' and 'azitawaddi' suggests the possibility that Aspendos was the city this king founded.

It fell to Croesus, king of Lydia, and then to the Persians in 547 BC, but seems to have retained a fair level of independence. By the beginning of the fifth century, Aspendos and Side were the only two towns to mint coins. Aspendos was situated on the banks of the River Eurymedon, now known as the Kopru Cay. In ancient times this was navigable; in fact, according to Strabo, the Persians anchored their ships there in 468 BC before the epic battle against the Delian Confederation led by Cimon with a fleet of two hundred ships. Later, in 467 BC, in order to crush to Persian land forces at Aspendos, Cimon tricked the Persians by sending his best fighters to shore wearing the garments of the hostages he had seized earlier. When they saw these men, the Persians thought that they were compatriots freed by the enemy and arranged festivities in celebration. Taking advantage of this, Cimon landed and annihilated the Persians.

Aspendos was occupied by Alexander the Great in 333 BC, who levied from there four thousand of 'the best horses in the world'. After his death it suffered several violent changes of rule. So it is no wonder that it opted to become an ally of Rome under the Kingdom of Pergamum after the Battle of Sipylum in 190 BC, and entered the Roman Empire in 133 BC. According to Cicero, it was plundered of many of its artistic treasures by the provincial governor Verres.

The town encompassed two hills: on the main hill stood the acropolis, with the agora, basilica, nymphaeum and bouleuterion or council chamber. Only ruins remain, including some rock-cut tombs of Phrygian design.

About one kilometre north of the town, one can still see the remains of the Roman aqueduct which supplied Aspendos with water, transporting it from a distance of over twelve miles, and which still maintains its original height. It represents an extraordinary feat of engineering and is one of the rare examples that still survive. The water was brought from the mountains in a channel formed by hollowed stone blocks on top of 15 metre-high arches. Near both ends of the aqueduct the water was collected in towers some 30 metres high, and then distributed to the city. An inscription found in Aspendos tells us that a certain Tiberius Claudius Italicus had the aqueduct built, and presented it to the city. Its architectural features and construction techniques date it to the middle of the second century AD.

Its theatre is the best preserved Roman theatre anywhere in Turkey. It was designed during the second century AD by the architect Zeno, son of Theodore and originally from Aspendos. Its two benefactors, the brothers Curtius Crispinus and Curtius Auspicatus, dedicated it to the Imperial family, as can be seen from certain engravings on the stones.

There is an amusing story, obviously not correct as it comes several centuries before, about the construction of this theatre and the aqueduct just outside the town. In ancient times, the King of Aspendos had a daughter of rare beauty named Semiramis, contended for marriage by two architects The king decided to give his daughter in marriage to the one who built an important public work in the shortest space of time. The two suitors thus got down to work and completed two public edifices at the same time: the theatre and the aquaduct. As the sovereign liked both buildings, he thought it right and just to divide his daughter in half. Whereas the designer of the aquaduct accepted the Solomonic division, the other preferred to grant the princess wholly to his rival. In this way, the sovereign understood that the designer of the theatre had not only built a magnificent theatre, but would also be an excellent husband to his daughter; consequently he granted him her hand in marriage.

The theatre is partially built into the slope of a hill. Today visitors enter the stage building by a door opened in the facade during a much later period. The original entrances, however, are the vaulted paradoses at both ends of the stage building. The cavea is semicircular in shape and divided in two by a large diazoma. There are twenty-one tiers of seats above and twenty below, each ninety-six metres long. To provide ease of circulation so that the spectators could reach their seats without difficulty, radiating stairways were built, ten in the lower level, starting at the orchestra, and twenty-one in the upper, beginning at the diazoma. A wide gallery consisting of fifty-nine arches, and thought to have been built at a later date, goes from one end of the upper cavea to the other. From an architectural point of view, the diazoma's vaulted gallery acts as a substructure supporting the upper cavea. As a general rule of protocol, the private boxes above the entrances on both sides of the cavea were reserved for the Imperial family and the vestal virgins. Beginning from the orchestra and going up, the first row of seats belonged to senators, judges, and ambassadors, while the second was reserved for other notables of the city. The remaining sections were open to all the citizens. The women usually sat on the upper rows under the gallery. From the names carved on certain seats in the upper cavea, it is clear that these too were reserved. Although it is impossible to determine the exact seating capacity of the theatre, in recent years, concerts given in the theatre as part of the Antalya Film and Art Festival have shown that as many as 20,000 spectators can be crowded into the seating area.

Without doubt the Aspendos theatre's most striking component is the stage building. On the lower floor of this two-storey structure, which is built of conglomerate rock, were five doors providing the actors' entrance to the stage. The large door at the centre was known as the porta regia, and the two smaller ones on either side as the porta hospitales. From surviving fragments it appears that sculptural works were placed in niches and aedicula under triangular and semicircular pediments.

In the pediment at the centre of the colonnaded upper floor is a relief of Dionysos, the god of wine and the founder and patron of theatres. Red zigzag motifs against white plaster, visible on some portions of the stage building, date to the Seljuk period when it was turned into a palace. The top of the stage building is covered with a highly ornamented wooden roof.

Lycia — historical notes

Lycia was and is a place with many assets, so it is not surprising that its history is one of invasion after invasion. The Greeks established some outposts and in 546 BC the Persians attacked Xanthos, the capital. Heroditus reports of a mass suicide rather than surrender.

> The Persian Army entered the plain of Xanthos under the command of Harpagos, and did battle with the Xanthians. The Xanthians fought with small numbers against the superior Persians forces, with legendary bravery. They resisted the endless Persian forces with great courage, but were finally beaten. They moved their womenfolk, children, slaves and treasures into the fortress. This was then set on fire from, below and around the walls , until destroyed by conflagration. Then the warriors of Xanthos made their final attack on the Persians, their voices raised in calls of war, until every last man from Xanthos was killed.

Excavations have revealed a thick layer of ash covering the site.

Persian rule in Lycia, as elsewhere, allowed considerable local autonomy. The economy flourished and the people appreciated their masters.

In 480 BC the Lycians contributed fifty ships to the Persian King Xerxes' invasion of Greece. Heroditus gives us this description:

> They wore greaves and corslets; they carried bows of cornel wood, cane arrows without feathers, and javelins. They had goatskins slung round their shoulders, and hats stuck round with feathers. They also carried daggers and rip-hooks.

A century later Lycia, by then under threat from the Carians, welcomed Alexander the Great. Lycia came under Ptolemaic rule for a century and adopted Greek, along with much of its culture, including a Greek constitution, and the cities joined the Lycian League. In 197 BC Lycia was taken by Antiochus III, king of Syria. He in turn was defeated by the Romans in 190 BC at the Battle of Magnesia. Lycia was put under Rhodes until they were granted semi-autonomy in 167 BC when the Roman Province of Asia was instituted.

Lycia remained loyal to Rome when in 88 BC the Pontic king Mithridates VI of Pontus tried to overthrow Roman rule. Rome showed its gratitude by extending Lycian territory.

When in 42 BC Brutus, during the Roman civil war, tried to take Xanthos, the people repeated the act of mass suicide made by their forebears five hundred years before. Brutus was defeated, and once more in gratitude Rome left Lycia the only country in the area free from direct rule. In AD 43 Claudius reduced Lycia to the status of a Roman province, and it was administered by a governor appointed by the emperor.

So Roman culture began to dominate city life: inscriptions show Roman names had been adopted, the emperor cult spread extensively, as did the Roman sports of gladiators and wild-animal fights. Vespasian and Hadrian visited and honoured the cities. Wealthy aristocrats built fine public buildings and trade expanded.

However, the earthquakes of AD 141 and 240 devastated many cities, and Lycia began to decline. After Constantine, Christianity spread rapidly in the area. In the eighth century Xanthos was made an archbishopric but was soon deserted in the face of Arab raids.

The whole area was sparsely populated until the nineteenth century when the Turks moved in Greeks from the Aegean islands as part of their aim to populate the islands with Turks. Eventually the Greeks were deported in 1922 in a series of population exchanges.

Throughout its history Lycia was known as the pirate coast. The many coves were ideal places to hide. It was not until 67 BC that Pompey was able to bring the situation under control. As Rome weakened, the area once more turned to piracy until the British navy in the eighteenth and nineteenth centuries finally destroyed their grip.

Patara

Patara is on the south-western coast facing Rhodes. It was one of Lycia's best harbours, serving as the port for the capital Xanthos. For most of its history it was free from the scourge of being a base for pirates. Shipping was protected by a headland forming a natural harbour and a lighthouse. Its value as a port was recognized from early times. Ptolemy Philadelphus (third century BC) enlarged the port and renamed it Arsinoe after his wife, a name it soon lost.

In Acts 21 Paul and his companions changed ships here, after leaving Rhodes en route for Tyre at the end of the Third Missionary journey in AD 57. At that time it seems to have been a place of reasonable size. Out of thirty-six members in the Lycian League, it was one of only six places which were able to elect three representatives to the council.

Not much is known of Patara's early history and there may well have been none, as it is not a site easily defensible. Around 440 BC coins begin to appear with the name Pttara. From then on its seems to have used the coins of the League, although sometimes minting its own, including low value coins in the time of the Roman empire.

Patara was well known in the ancient world for the worship of Apollo. Roman and Greek poets make reference to the god as one who spoke in oracles only during the winter months, as he went to Delos for the summer! Homer wrote of Apollo, 'O Lord, Lycia is yours, charming city by the sea, but over wave-girt Delos you greatly reign your own self'.

The ruins are extensive and in recent years many tons of sand have been cleared to reveal even more of Patara's treasures.

The triple-arched gateway was built in AD 100 by the Roman governor Mettius Modestus. There are many niches and plinths for statues of the family members.

The theatre dates back to early times but was rebuilt by Velia Procula and her father in AD 147. It has 34 rows and may have held an audience of around 10,000.

Close to the theatre is a structure that seated around 500 and may have been used as an Odeon or council chamber.

From the top to the theatre it is possible to see the outline of the harbour and on the far side the large ruins of Hadrian's Granary — a reminder of Paul's time — when this was a transhipment port of grain from the east to Rome. The granary measured 67 by 19 metres and was divided into eight storehouses.

There are also Lycian and Roman tombs and baths. Christianity took a while to establish itself. It was the birthplace of St Nicholas and there are remains of a seventh-century basilica.

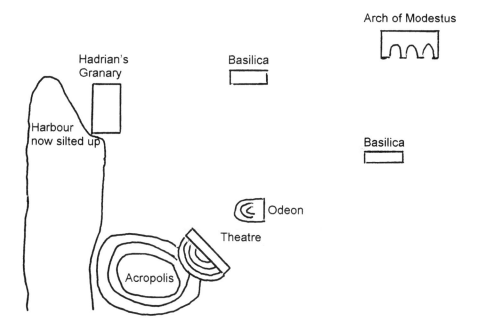

Sketch plan of Patara

Xanthos

Xanthos is the former capital of Lycia. Part of its history is described in the notes on the history of Lycia, most notably the two occasions on which it was destroyed by fire in 546 BC and 42 BC.

The ruins lie on a plateau, high above the left bank of the river. It is possible to make out the plan of the city with its walls and gates. Many of the greatest treasures of the site were shipped by Sir Charles Fellows to the British Museum (some of these can be seen by searching under Xanthos on www.thebritishmuseum.ac.uk/compass).

The theatre is well preserved and is remarkable for a break in the curve of its auditorium, which was constructed so as not to interfere with the two pillar tombs eight metres high. The 'Harpy monument' still stands to its full height. Although the original reliefs are now in the British Museum, good quality plaster copies are in their place showing harpies — half-bird, half-woman spirits carrying off the dead. Others interpret the reliefs as portraying the husband and wife receiving the homage of sirens. Beside this first century Roman tomb is one from the Lycian period.

To the north of the agora stands the famous stele of Xanthus, inscribed on all four sides in Lycian and Greek. It is the longest Lycian inscription known. Linguistically it falls into three parts: beginning on the south side, it continues onto the east side and part of the north side in the normal Lycian language. It then follows with a twelve-lined poem in Greek, but the rest of the north side and the whole of the west side is filled with a strange form of Lycian, perhaps ceremonial, which appears elsewhere only on a tomb in Antiphellos. This inscription is believed to be a narrative account of the dead hero's exploits possibly defending their territory from the Athenians during the Peloponesian wars.

Behind the theatre is a terrace on which probably the temple of either the Xanthian Apollo or Sarpedon stood. The best of the tombs — the Payava tomb, the Nereid monument, the Ionic monument and the Lion tomb — are in the British Museum.

A fine triple gateway, much polygonal masonry, and the walls of the acropolis are the other objects of most interest.

Across the car park is a large a Byzantine basilica with a mosaic floor, and a baptistery at the Northeast corner. It was built in the time of Justinian around AD 530. Further on is a tomb depicting a warrior in action and further up the acropolis are other tombs including the plinth for the tomb of Payana which is now in the British Museum. On the top of the hill are the remains of a monastery and Roman temple.

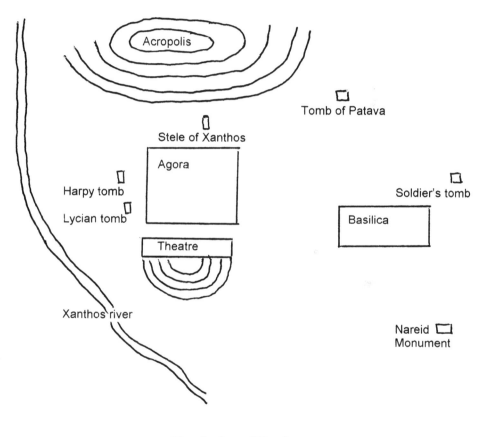

Sketch plan of Xanthos

Myra

Myra — the name means myrrh — was a major city in the Lycian Union. Constantine made it the capital of Lycia.

Paul visited Myra, as Luke recounts in Acts 27:

> When we had sailed across the open sea off the coast of Cilicia and Pamphylia, we landed at Myra in Lycia. There the centurion found an Alexandrian ship sailing for Italy and put us on board.

Little is known of its early history but some of the defensive walls date back to the fifth century BC. As a member of the Lycian League it was granted three representatives and so was among the six most important cities.

It grew in importance when the trade with Egypt opened up, with the larger ships taking a direct route from Alexandra to Andiake, the port of Myra, by skirting west of Cyprus. One of these ships, hired by the centurion, was to end up wrecked off the coast of Malta. On leaving Alexandra the ships could not sail on a direct course further to the west, as the prevailing wind in the east Mediterranean is from a westerly direction. However, once at Myra, they could reach Italy by following the coast and using local winds blowing off the many islands.

Sailors would fulfil their vows to their god on reaching Myra, and that is one reason why in the Christian era St Nicholas became the patron saint of sailors. By the eleventh century AD Myra was deserted and its port disappeared into the sand.

Myra's theatre is the largest theatre in Lycia. Its double-vaulted corridors are still preserved, in one on the west side is an inscription that seems to be a reserved place for a local trader and his wares. There are only six rows of seats above the diazoma and 29 below. An inscription in a stall marks the seat of a shopkeeper Gelasius. The ruins of the stage have been unearthed revealing a frieze with actors' masks and the Roman Corinthian capitals. On the way out of the theatre by the stage door it is possible to see a cross section of the debris that covered the site for many centuries. It is thought that there was a major earthquake and the tsunami swept up the valley with a large deposit of shingle blocking

74

the river which formed into a large lake. The result was around two metres of gravel from the sea with a similar thickness above of river mud.

The steep cliff behind the theatre leads up to the acropolis with the remains of walls from the Lycian period. The cliff contains a large number of rock-cut tombs. Most of them are from the fourth century BC, and many contain reliefs of the life of the deceased as well as of the funeral. One tomb shows the deceased with his family perhaps at the last supper before his death. Another at ground level show two warriors. There is another group of tombs further up the valley. In the mid-nineteenth century many of the tombs were painted red, yellow and blue. The colour no longer exists which may indicate that it had been put on at a later date when they were used as homes.

The port of Myra, Andriache is five kilometres down the valley and still in a large area of swamp before the river runs through to the sea at the present port. To the south of the swamp are the ruins of Hadrian's Granary. There is a bust of Hadrian and his empress at the main portal.

Cities and their ports

Luke, in Acts, usually mentions the ports of departure. So, for instance, he points out in Acts 13:4 that Paul sailed from Seleucia. In Acts 21:1 he points out that Paul landed and sailed from Patara. No mention is made of the city of Xanthos, of which Patara was the port. It is possible that Paul, in his haste to reach Jerusalem, found a ship in Patara leaving so soon after his arrival that he did not have time to visit Xanthos. We have the opposite situation with Andiache and Myra in Acts 27:6. There the port is not mentioned. It is possible that on arrival Paul and his guard went straight to the city of Myra, where there was a garrison, and stayed there while the centurion searched for a ship sailing for Italy.

St Nicholas

St Nicholas was born in Patara. His wealthy parents died of plague in his childhood. He inherited an estate which enabled him to make pilgrimages to Egypt and Palestine and carry out charitable work.

He was made bishop of the newly formed diocese of Myra by Constantine. At the Council of Nicea he is reputed to have physically attacked Arius. That may not have been his only fight, as his skull reveals that at some stage he broke his nose.

He died between AD 340 and 350. In the sixth century the church of St Nicholas was built round his tomb. The sarcophagus is still there, but the bones were taken in the eleventh century by sailors sent from Bari in Italy, to provide a relic to rival those of other Italian cities like the bones of St Mark in Venice. It is said that upon smashing the lid of the tomb the thieves were almost overcome by the glowing bones and the powerful smell of myrrh. In 1862 Czar Alexander of Russia began a renovation of the church and further work has been carried out by the Turkish government.

His link with Santa Claus comes from a very early story that, on hearing that a shopkeeper was too poor to supply his daughters with dowries, he went by night and threw three bags of gold down the chimney or through the window or into the yard. At least by some means his gift saved the girls from a life of prostitution. Later these three golden bags or balls were used as the symbol of a pawnbroker's shop. It is thought that the idea of giving anonymous gifts was first adopted in the West by French nuns who left stockings for the poor, filled with fruit and nuts.

Myra is a centre of a large pilgrimage each year on 6 December. On that day, in countries like Germany, Switzerland and the Netherlands, gifts are given to children. St Nicholas is also regarded in high esteem in Russia and, as Lapland was once part of that country, may be the reason why his present home is in Lapland!

At the Reformation, customs linked to saints and their relics were banned, and in many Protestant countries this ban included the keeping of the feast of St Nicholas on 6 December. To observe English law the traditions were moved to 25 December, although many of these were banned at the time of the Commonwealth.

The customary Santa Claus was brought to England through the paintings by Bret Harte depicting the customs of the Dutch living in New Amsterdam. But its main boost came with a major advertising campaign by Coca Cola which featured the traditionally dressed Santa Claus. Maybe it is appropriate that the custom of spending large sums of money on Christmas presents should come from what is often seen the commercial centre of the West — New York — and a well-known multinational company. The spending spree associated with Christmas has grown larger in recent times. Of course, if we are to follow the example of St Nicholas, our focus should be anonymous gifts to the poor!

In the Middle Ages at least four hundred English churches were dedicated to his name. In those days he was mainly regarded as the patron saint of sailors, and also of prisoners as he had been imprisoned in the reign of Diocletian and is reputed to have turned many thieves from their evil ways.

Islam

Most Muslims follow Sunni Islam. However Islam is divided just as much as Christianity into various denominations. A major one is the Shi'ite: Iran, Azerbaijan, Iraq. Just as there are many nominal Christians who are a bad example of our faith, so there are many Muslims who claim to be followers because they live in a Muslim country but who are just as nominal.

Five basic duties or pillars

Shahadah: declaration of faith by reciting 'There is not god but Allah, Muhammad is the messenger of Allah.'

Salah: five compulsory daily prayers at *fajr*, around dawn; *zuhr*, after midday; *asr*, just before sunset; *maghrib*, after sunset; *isha*, at night.

Zakah: welfare contribution of 5-10% on agricultural produce, at various rates for livestock and 2.5% of the value of jewellery, cash at bank and trading goods.

Hajj: pilgrimage to Mecca This is usually undertaken once in a lifetime and in old age, as it is linked with forgiveness of sins.

Sawm: fasting during Ramadan. This fast is from dawn to sunset in the ninth month. Food and drink are taken outside this time.

Call to prayer

اَللّٰهُ اَكْبَرُ   Allahu Akbar — Allah is the greatest

اَشْهَدُ اَنْ لَااِلٰهَ اِلَّا اللّٰهُ   Ashhadu an la ilaha illallah — I bear witness that there is no god but Allah

اَشْهَدُ اَنَّ مُحَمَّدًا رَسُوْلُ اللّٰهِ   Ashhadu anna muhammadar rasulullar I bear witness that Muhammed is Allah's messenger

حَىَّ عَلَى الصَّلٰوةِ   Hayya alas salah — Rush to prayer

حَىَّ عَلَى الْفَلَاحِ   Hayya alal falah — Rush to success

اَللّٰهُ اَكْبَرُ   Allahu Akbar — Allah is the greatest

لَااِلٰهَ اِلَّا اللّٰهُ   La ilaha illal lah — There is no god but Allah.

The first phrase is repeated four times. All others are repeated twice except the last phrase, which is said only once.

Basic beliefs are grouped under

Tawhid: this is the belief that Allah is one, eternal and absolute. Everything in the universe has a set, predetermined course called Al-Qadr.

Risalah: these are the channels of communication between Allah and ourselves. There are the angels, heavenly servants of Allah; messengers or prophets (listed below) and books of Allah the Tawrat, torah of Moses; the Zabur, psalms of David; Injil, gospel of Jesus; and the Quran revealed to Muhammad. It is claimed that the Quran is pure and unchanged whereas the other books that are in the Bible have been changed by Jews and Christians from the pure words of God.

Akhirah: day of judgment by Allah, and then eternal life after death in heaven or hell.

Prophets

The Quran mentions the 25 most important prophets as
(quranic name followed by biblical name where appropriate):
Adam – Adam; Idris – Enoch; Nuh – Noah; Hud; Salih; Ibrahim – Abraham; Isma'il – Ishmael; Ishaq – Isaac; Lut – Lot; Yaqub – Jacob; Yusuf – Joseph; Shu'aib; Ayyub – Job; Musa – Moses; Harun – Aaron; Dhu'l-kifl – Ezekiel; Dawud – David; Sulaiman – Solomon; Ilias – Elijah; Al-Yasa – Elisha; Yunus – Jonah; Zakariyya – Zechariah; Yahya – John; Isa – Jesus; Muhammad.

Muhammad

As a boy of 12 Muhammad went with his uncle on a business trip to Syria. At Bozra they were invited into the home of a Christian priest called Bahira, who recognized Muhammad's potential. At 25 he married a rich widow Khadijah, aged 40, and they had six children. He spent much time in meditation and prayer as well as being active in helping to repair the Kabah at Mecca. Khadijah's cousin had a knowledge of the Bible but like many of that time had strayed a long way from it. Muhammad rightly revolted against these corrupt practices. Allah revealed to him by his angel the true faith, and in 612 AD the Islamic movement began.

Icons

Icons are a key feature within the Orthodox Churches. The word *icon* comes from the Greek *eikon* — a likeness. Paul speaks of Christ as in the likeness of God. So if we want to know what God is like, we look at Jesus. In the west, our art is mainly in stained-glass windows. In the east, where persecution has always been part of their life, their art was concentrated in an object that could easily be removed and hidden. Like the church stained-glass windows, the icon has the purpose of creating a sense of reverence, of instructing those unable to read, and helping the worshipper draw closer to God. It is important to realize that the Orthodox Christians do not worship the icon any more than we worship the art in our own churches.

Icons are not photographs: they are paintings that invite us to meet Christ through the events that really happened and people who really lived. They are symbols of God's presence in our world. That is why they always feature real people. In the icon, the central figure — usually Jesus Christ or Mary or a saint — is always the largest. This is a way of focusing our minds on the central character.

The background of icons is gold, a colour that symbolizes the glory of heaven. There are no shadows because heaven's glory shines on all, revealing their truth and beauty. If a dark area exists, then it is dispelled by Christ, the light of the world.

Colours are very significant. White and gold are Christ's colours. As an adult, Christ often wears a red inner garment covered by a blue cloak. Red is a sign of Christ's divinity and blue is a sign of his humanity. He is God but he takes on our human flesh. These colours are reversed for the Virgin Mary. Her inner robe is blue (human) but covered with a cloak of red (divine).

Most icons draw our eyes towards the 'Christ' figure. They remind us the he is the centre of our faith. Christ must lead us on our journey; through him and with him we must make our way to heaven; others in the picture are our companions — our friends who help us along the path, for we never travel alone.

We now look at three of these icons and draw out their meaning.

Pantocrator

Here Christ reigns on his heavenly throne. As the Son is in the *eikon* of the Father, in his face we see the Father as well. It is an icon of the almighty God. This is an icon  of the long years of persecution when Islam threatened the whole future of the church. It emphasizes God enthroned as the supreme ruler, surrounded by saints and angels.

The word *pantocrator* comes in Revelation 1:8, where God says 'I am the Alpha and the Omega, who is, and who was, and who is to come, the *pantocrator* [almighty]'.

The use of a multicoloured band around God is based on Revelation 4:3 where the rainbow surrounds the throne of God.

The book is closed, for God alone knows those who are written in his book of life (Rev. 3:5 et al.).

Theotokos

No human model can be found to show the holiness of the Virgin Mary, so an idealized form is created for her. Looking at this icon, our thoughts are concentrated on her face, and especially the eyes that show her virtues of meekness, purity, humility and love.

This icon of the Incarnation has within it some special features. We note that Mary does not look at Jesus, nor ourselves, nor even into the distance. Instead, her eyes are a channel to look deep inside her. She contemplates the mystery of God become man. Her tenderness is expressed in the shyness of her hands, which can hardly bear to hold the Christ-child. Human love is expressed in Jesus. He shows God's love and tenderness to one who is not only his mother but his creature.

81

The Dormition

Another icon is of the falling asleep of the Virgin Mary. Behind her stands Jesus, holding in his arms a tiny infant, which is her soul newly born into eternal life. A pagan figure in front tries to upset her coffin and an angel comes to protect her, which is a symbolic comment on the Council of Ephesus, when the church disputed on how Mary carried within her the divine nature as well as the human nature of Jesus.

Icons - some key points

a)   The icon is theology in picture.   It stresses the incarnation: God became man in Jesus. To deny this is to deny the very basis of faith.

b) The icon seeks to portray the two natures of Jesus: human and divine. Icons of the saints portray a glorified state of one who has been made holy by God.

c)   An icon portrays what happens to people after God touches them. Filled with the Holy Spirit, the physical body is transformed and becomes like the spiritual body which we receive at the Second Coming.

d)   The icon is present in every Orthodox home.   It transforms each home into a place where we live in the presence of God and he is listening to our prayers.

e)   Icon painters have traditionally been monks who have prepared themselves for the painting of each icon through fasting, prayer, and the Holy Communion.

f) The best icon of God is men and women who are made in God's own *eikon.* That is why, in Orthodox worship, after the priest has censed the icons, he turns and censes the people.

g) The whole Bible is about this *eikon* of God in man: how the likeness was marred by sin and how Jesus came to restore the *eikon* of God in each one of us.   Through the icon we remind ourselves of this.   Our spiritual journey is to enter God's family and then be changed into his likeness. 'And we, who with unveiled faces all reflect the Lord's glory, are being transformed into his likeness with ever-increasing glory, which comes from the Lord, who is the Spirit' (II Cor. 3:18).

Some early Christian symbols

The fish   The Greek word for a fish is ichthus ιχθυς. The letters stand for the first letters of the Greek words for

Jesus	-	Ιησους
Christ	-	Χριστος
God's	-	Θεος
Son	-	Υιος
Saviour	-	Σωτηρ

In Ephesus we will see a more complicated symbol dating from the second century that is made up using the same words in this way.

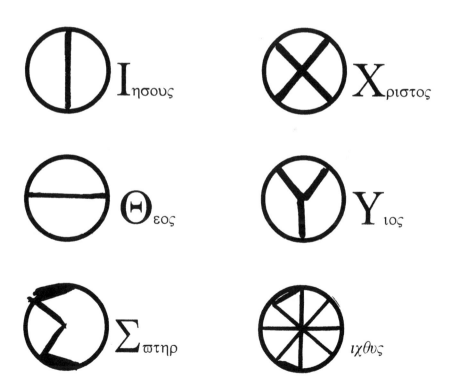

The Greek alphabet

Name	capital	lower case	like English
Alpha	A	α	a
Beta	B	β	b
Gamma	Γ	γ	g
Delta	Δ	δ	d
Epsilon	E	ε	e
Zeta	Z	ζ	z
Eta	H	η	e as in fete
Theta	Θ	θ	th
Iota	I	ι	i
Kappa	K	κ	k
Lambda	Λ	λ	l
Mu	M	μ	m
Nu	N	ν	n
Xi	Ξ	ξ	x
Omicron	O	o	o
Pi	Π	π	p
Rho	P	ρ	r
Sigma	Σ	σ ς	s
Tau	T	τ	t
Upsilon	Y	υ	u
Phi	Φ	φ	ph
Chi	X	χ	ch
Psi	Ψ	ψ	ps
Omega	Ω	ω	o as in tone